50 Nature
Cross-Stitch Designs

STEP-BY-STEP

50 Nature
Cross-Stitch Designs

Lynda Burgess

Photographs by Amanda Heywood

SMITHMARK

MW

This edition published in 1996 by
Smithmark Publishers, a division of U.S. Media Holdings, Inc.,
16 East 32nd Street, New York, NY 10016.

SMITHMARK books are available for bulk purchase for sales promotion and for
premium use. For details write or call the manager of special sales, SMITHMARK
Publishers 16 East 32nd Street, New York, 10016; (212) 532-6600

Produced by Anness Publishing Limited
1 Boundary Row
London SE1 8HP

Printed and bound in Hong Kong

10 9 8 7 6 5 4 3 2 1

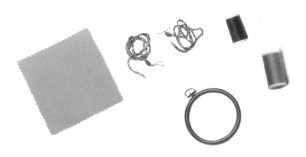

CONTENTS

INTRODUCTION

Everyone yearns to be creative, but not everyone is confident that they have the necessary skills and ability. Cross stitch is a great pastime because it gives people who long to create the opportunity to be artistic – even if they don't feel they have a wealth of artistic talent. If you can master the simple cross stitches and follow a chart, you can make beautiful pictures that will last a lifetime and become heirlooms for future generations. It couldn't be easier. This book is a library of 50 nature and wildlife designs for cross stitchers of all levels of ability. Whether you're just a beginner or a more accomplished and experienced stitcher, you're sure to find something you'll want to stitch. And if as a beginner you want to try one of the more complicated projects, don't worry, the step-by-step instructions will take you through any stitch or method that may seem a little difficult.

Before you start stitching, there are a couple of things to consider. To ensure perfect pictures every time, make sure that all the stitches run in the same direction. Do not pull the stitches too tight. When working stitches to the left, pull the needle towards your left shoulder and when working stitches to the right, pull towards the right. Many stitchers find that hours of continuous stitching cause their shoulders to start aching. To avoid this, work with a lamp behind your stitching shoulder – the heat from the light keeps the muscles warm – and be sure to stretch your shoulder muscles every half-hour.

All projects are worked in Anchor threads, although colour descriptions are given in each key so that you can work with your own threads and match the colours. In some projects, a sewing machine has been used, although every design that calls for a machine can also be made up by hand.

There's a wealth of design ideas to keep nature lovers occupied. As you leaf through the pages and decide on your first project, you're just beginning hours of enjoyable and creative cross stitching.

Materials

A variety of materials are used in this book, all of which should be available from your local craft stockist, but if not, try one of the suppliers listed at the back of the book.

Aida
This is the most popular fabric for cross stitch. It is a cotton fabric available in a variety of colours. There are holes between the warp (vertical) and weft (horizontal) threads into which you make your cross stitches. Fabric sizes are designated by the number of holes per inch, for example, 14 holes per inch (hpi) will give you 14 stitches every inch of fabric. The most common counts of Aida in the shops are 11, 14, 16, 18 and 22. The easiest to work on is probably 14 hpi as the holes are easy to see and your work grows fairly quickly.

Aida plus
This is a relatively new, sturdy fabric with a paper-like quality, ideal for bookmarks and projects that require moulding, folding and cutting. Available in 14 hpi.

Aida band
This is ideal for making a cross-stitch border to add to a towel or curtain. It is available in widths from 2.5 to 10 cm (1 to 4 in) and a range of colours.

Aida tea towel
This is a standard kitchen tea towel with an Aida band woven across one edge, creating an original and practical towel.

Evenweave
As the name suggests, the warp and the weft threads of this fabric are equidistant, forming small squares or blocks of holes around the threads. The stitches are worked into the holes, either across a single thread or, more commonly in cross stitch, two threads. Many of the projects in this book are worked over two threads on a 28 hpi evenweave.

Felt
This bonded fabric is ideal for backing your work as it does not fray. It is generally available in 18 cm (7 in) squares and in a wide range of colours.

Waste canvas
This is used for stitching a design on to a ready-made garment. Tack (baste) the canvas on to the garment, then stitch the design through both canvas and fabric. After completion, dampen slightly; the starch in the waste canvas dissolves and you can remove the threads.

Stranded cottons
The most common threads used for cross stitch are stranded cottons or embroidery floss. Each skein is made up of six stranded threads which can be separated. Most of the projects described in this book are worked in two strands.

Marlitt threads
These have a lustre and give your work an attractive, silky appearance, ideal for enhancing a motif design.

Kreinik blending filaments
Formerly known as Balger, Kreinik threads are sold as single strands on a card or bobbin. The threads look luxurious, with metallic blends of gold, silver, red, green and blue – ideal for adding dramatic detail.

Metallic threads
These are coarser than blending filaments and come in a variety of thicknesses. Although they can be used for cross stitch, they do not blend very well with the embroidery threads (floss).

Sewing threads
The sewing threads in the book are polyester threads. They are strong and work well on all sewing machines.

Beads
Work the first part of a half cross stitch and thread the bead on to the needle before inserting it back into the fabric to complete the half cross stitch. Beads are available from most craft shops in a variety of lustrous colours. You may prefer using a beading needle, which has a small head and a long, thin needle point.

Interfacing
This is a bonded fabric used to give support and stiffness, and to help to prevent distortion. It is available in sew-in or iron-on forms in a range of weights.

Wadding (Batting)
This is used to lift work when mounting it in cards, pots and frames. Wadding placed behind your work will keep the stitches plush and show them to their best advantage. It comes in a variety of weights; for cross stitch we recommend you use a 50 g (2 oz) wadding.

Aida

evenweave

ribbon

velcro

wadding
(batting)

fabric

beads

backing
and lining
fabric

piping cord

sewing
thread

stranded
cotton

interfacing

metallic
thread

felt

thread

metallic
thread

cotton tape

Aida

ribbon

zip (zipper)

Aida bands

Equipment

None of the equipment needed for cross stitch is bulky or heavy. Its portability is one reason why cross stitch is such a great hobby. You can do it anywhere. Once you have these few essential items to hand, you'll be ready to cross stitch.

All-purpose scissors
A sharp pair of all-purpose scissors is a good investment. Be sure to keep them for cutting fabric only, as anything else will dull the blades. A 13 cm (5 in) blade is excellent for most things. It is a good idea to buy a second, less expensive pair for slightly tougher tasks of cutting card, threads and tape, and in this way you will extend the life of both pairs.

Embroidery scissors
Embroidery scissors differ from ordinary, all-purpose scissors because the blades have sharp pointed tips, which enable you to cut behind stitches without cutting into the fabric. They are small and fit neatly into a handbag or work bag.

Snips
The primary purpose of these tiny clippers is snipping any stray threads. They are made of two facing blades, which are held together by a piece of strong wire. Like embroidery scissors, they fit neatly into a handbag or work bag.

Pins
Make sure you always use stainless steel pins because they do not rust. Rust marks on your work can be difficult to remove. Extra-fine long pins are the best, because they will not make lasting holes when pinning your work together. There are a variety of pins available, from gold-plated ones, which do not mark light-coloured fabric, to glass-headed pins which are easy to find.

Tapestry needles
Tapestry needles have a blunt end and a large eye. They come in a range of sizes. The most commonly used are 22, 24 and 26. The higher the number, the finer the needle. When working with a higher count fabric, it is advisable to use a finer needle. Most of the projects in the book call for a size 26.

Sharp needles
These needles, used for hand sewing, are long and have a fine sharp end. A longer needle is easy to manipulate in and out of the fabric and, being fine, it will not leave unsightly holes or marks in the fabric.

Tape measure
You can buy tape measures with both metric and imperial measurements. A plastic-coated measure is better than a cloth one, because with constant use the cloth tends to stretch out of shape so its measurements are not always as accurate as they should be. Use your tape measure for checking seam allowances and sizes of fabric.

Ruler
It you want a good ruler to use for your cross-stitch project, consider using a stainless steel one. A great advantage of a metal ruler is that it has a straight edge without any pitting. When you are cutting a straight edge of card or through layers of fabric, it is important that your ruler has a smooth edge. You can buy rulers with both metric and imperial measurements.

Double-sided tape
Double-sided tape is an absolute joy to have when making up cross-stitch projects. It is clean and wonderfully easy to use. You simply fix one side to your work, pull away the backing tape and join your surfaces together. It is especially good to use for putting together cards.

Pencil
You may need a pencil to mark out your projects. There are several different types of pencil you could choose. A fabric marker will disappear when you wash your fabric. For the projects in this book we have used a soft drawing pencil, worked lightly over the fabric. If you use it lightly it will leave only a faint mark which will not show on your finished work. However, if any marks can be seen, they are easy to wash off.

Tailor's chalk
Tailor's chalk is used for marking fabric. It comes in a variety of pale colours. You use the chalk to draw around templates and it leaves a light mark on the fabric. You should be able to brush the chalk away quite easily with a soft brush when you've finished working.

all-purpose scissors

snips

embroidery scissors

glue

seam ripper

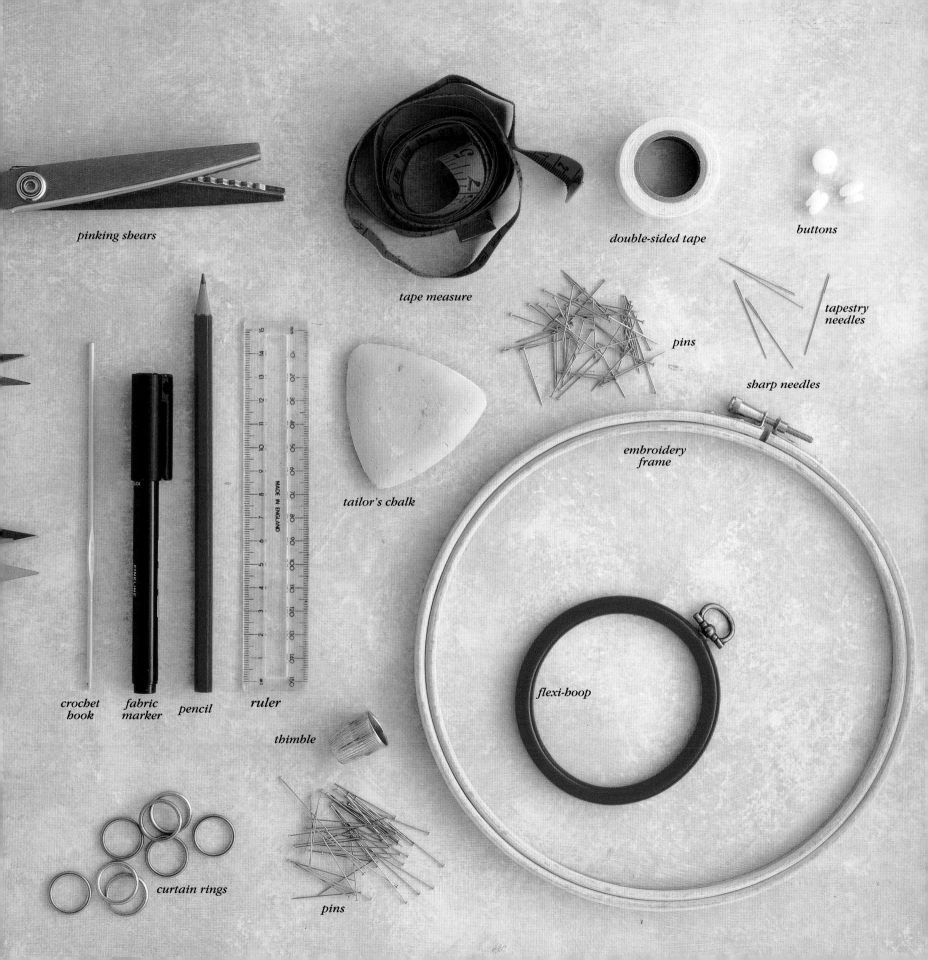

pinking shears

tape measure

double-sided tape

buttons

tapestry needles

pins

sharp needles

tailor's chalk

embroidery frame

crochet hook

fabric marker

pencil

ruler

MADE IN ENGLAND

flexi-hoop

thimble

curtain rings

pins

TECHNIQUES

Cross stitch

If you want to become a cross-stitch expert, you should first master this simple stitch. It is the basic stitch from which all cross-stitch pictures are made.

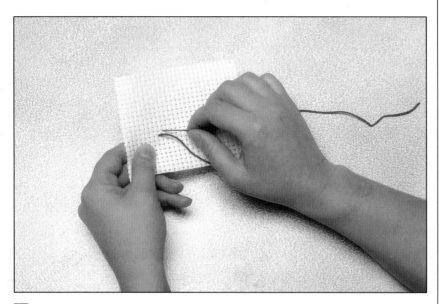

1 To make a cross stitch, first bring your needle up through the fabric in the bottom left-hand corner where you want the stitch to begin. Drop the needle back through the fabric in the top right-hand corner to make a diagonal stitch.

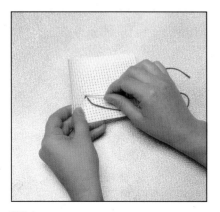

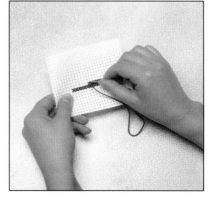

2 Bring the needle up through the fabric at the bottom right and drop it back through at the top left to complete the cross stitch.

3 Repeat these steps to make a row of stitches.

Continuous cross stitch

If you're working large areas in a single colour, this method of creating cross stitches will save you both time and unnecessary effort.

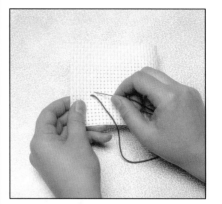

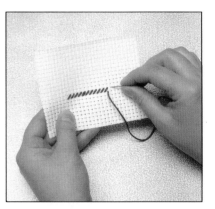

1 To make a cross stitch, take your needle up through the fabric in the bottom left-hand corner where you want the stitch to be. Drop the needle back through the fabric in the top right-hand corner to make a diagonal stitch.

2 Bring the needle up at the bottom right-hand corner of the first stitch and, moving towards the right, drop it back through the fabric in the following top right-hand corner. Repeat this step to form a row of half cross stitches.

3 Turn the needle around, bringing it up through the fabric in the bottom right-hand corner and dropping it down at the top left. Repeat this step to finish off your crosses.

Half cross stitch

Sometimes a design may use a half cross stitch instead of a full one. Make one simply by working half a stitch. It is often used where the work requires a lighter touch.

1 First consider where you want to start stitching. Then, to make a half cross stitch, bring the needle through the fabric in the bottom left-hand corner of the stitch.

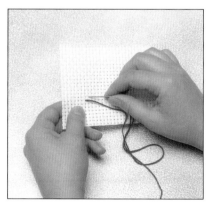

2 Moving towards the right, drop the needle back through the fabric in the following top right-hand corner to make a diagonal stitch.

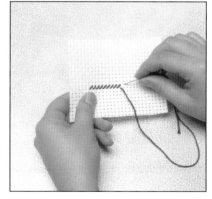

3 Repeat this step to form a row of half cross stitches.

Three-quarter stitch

When working a design, you may find that an area requires part of a stitch to be worked in one colour and the rest in a second colour. Look closely at your work to judge where the three-quarter stitch and the quarter stitch should lie.

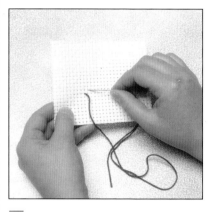 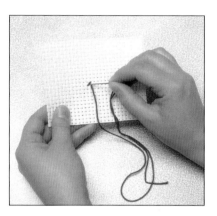

1 Bring the needle up through the fabric in the bottom left-hand corner of the stitch. Drop the needle back through the fabric in the top right-hand corner to make a diagonal stitch.

2 Bring the needle back through the fabric at the bottom right and drop it back halfway, directly in the middle of the stitch.

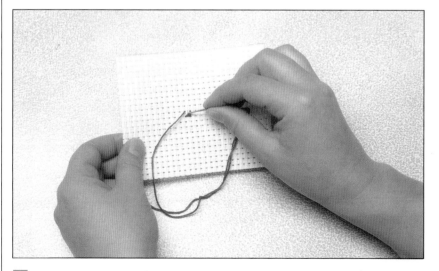

3 Change to a second colour of thread and bring the needle up through the fabric at the top left of the stitch. Drop it back through the fabric to meet the first colour in the middle of the stitch. This will complete your three-quarter stitch.

Long stitch

Long stitch can be used to add detail to your work. Although it is not used in all projects, it is a useful stitch to master should you wish to add some of your own definition.

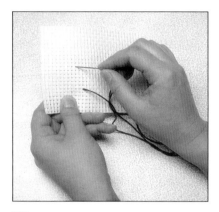 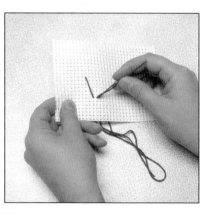

1 Bring the needle up through the fabric where you want the long stitch to begin.

2 Taking your needle across the fabric, drop it back through where you want the stitch to end. Pull the thread firmly but not too tightly.

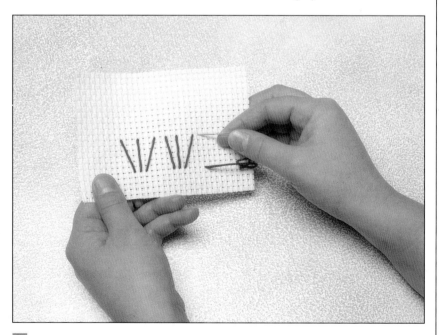

3 Repeat these steps, bringing the needle up through the fabric where you want the next stitch to start.

Backstitch

Used for outlining, backstitch is an essential stitch to master. By following the instructions below, you'll be an expert in minutes.

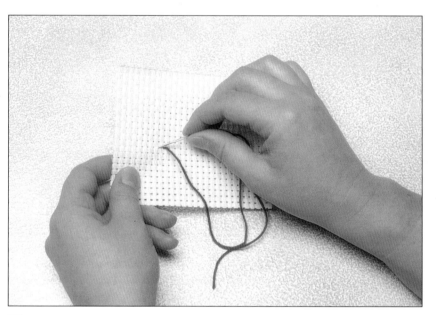

1 Bring the needle up through the fabric one hole ahead of where you want the stitch to begin. Drop the needle into the previous hole, bringing it up again one hole ahead of your original stitch.

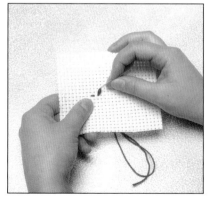 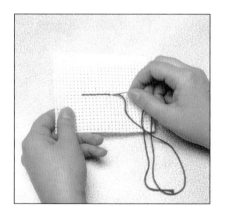

2 Drop the needle back through the fabric into the previous stitch and bring it up one hole ahead.

3 Repeat these steps to complete a row of backstitch.

French knot

French knots are created by wrapping the thread around the needle and pulling the needle back through the fabric. The textured knots are ideal for flower centres and for the middle of an animal's eye.

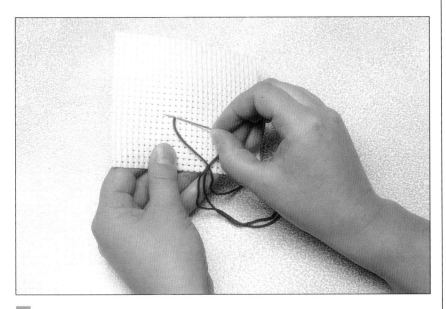

1 Bring the needle up through the fabric where you want the stitch to begin, then make a small stitch in the fabric but do not pull the needle out of the fabric.

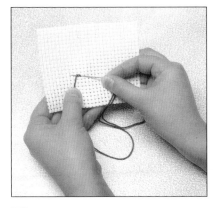

2 Wrap the thread twice around the needle and pull the needle through the loops, ensuring the loops work towards the end of the thread close to the fabric.

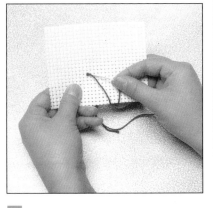

3 Drop the needle back through the fabric close to the knot and finish off on the underside.

Holbein stitch

Holbein stitch is an alternative to backstitch used for outlining your work. It is worked by making a running stitch, turning your work and filling the gaps as you work back to the starting point.

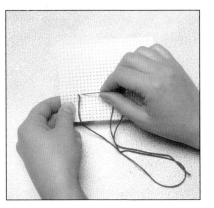

1 Bring the needle up through the fabric where you want the stitch to begin and drop it into the next hole to the right.

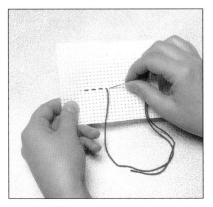

2 Continue in a running stitch, bringing the needle up and down into every other hole.

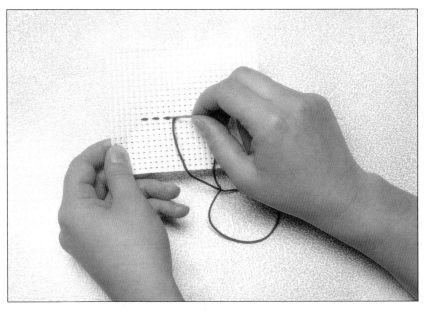

3 When you have worked a running stitch outline, turn the work around and sew a running stitch in the other direction, to fill the alternate gaps.

Lacing a picture

When you've finished stitching, you may decide to mount your work in a frame. You could send it to a framer but, by following the simple steps detailed below, you can prepare the picture for framing yourself.

1 Cut a piece of cardboard and a piece of wadding (batting) the same size as you want the finished framed work to be. With the design facing down, centre the wadding and then the card on the back of the work.

2 Fold over the top and bottom edges of the work, pinning them along the grain of the fabric to the top and bottom of the cardboard.

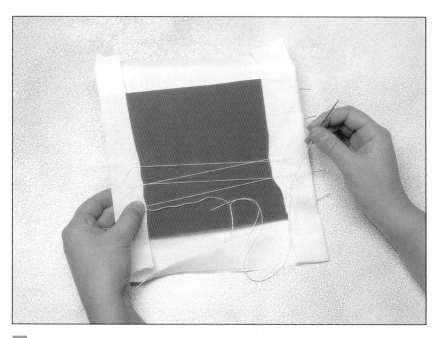

3 Starting from the centre, use lacing thread to work a herringbone stitch from side to side towards the bottom edge. Pull the sides tightly together. Repeat this step, working from the centre to the top edge.

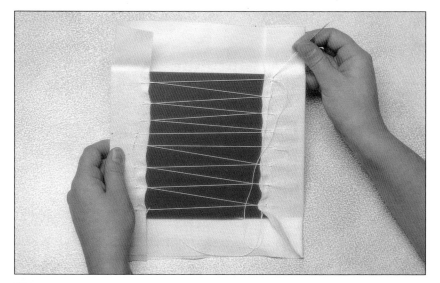

4 Fold over the long edges, mitring the corners to keep them neat.

5 Repeat the lacing process on the long edges.

6 Finish the work by slip stitching the corners, and place it in a picture frame.

Filling a pot

Several of the projects in this book have been mounted in craft pots. This is a popular and easy mount for cross-stitch projects and pots are widely available in all good craft shops.

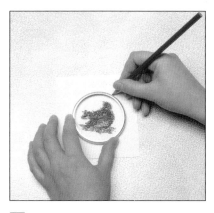

1 With the stitching face down, centre the lid over it and use a pencil to draw around it on the back of the work.

2 Cut around the pencil line. This will leave you with a design that will fit inside your pot.

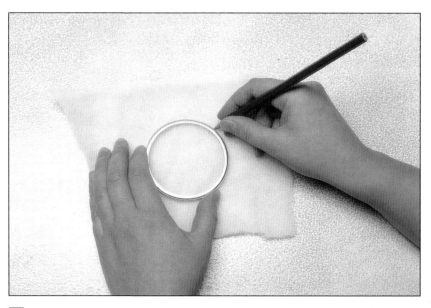

3 Draw around the lid of the pot on to a piece of wadding (batting).

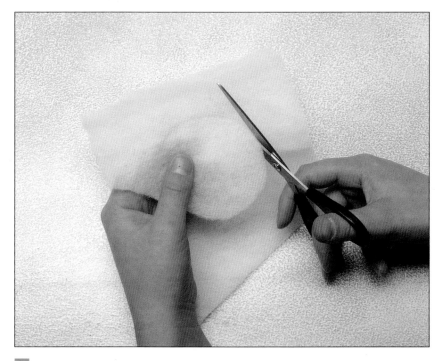

4 Cut out the circle from the wadding (batting).

5 Position the design inside the rim, with the embroidery facing into the lid. Place the wadding (batting) on top.

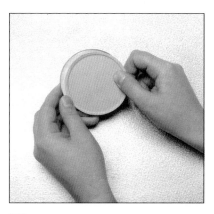

6 Fix the metal disk over both the design and the wadding (batting) to hold them firmly in place.

Filling a card

Once you have learned how to put your work into a card, you'll never be at a loss for a cross-stitch mount and your friends will love their personalized greetings.

1 Use a pencil to draw around the card opening on to the wadding (batting).

2 Cut around the pencil line.

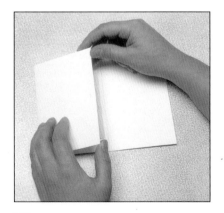

3 Trim the edges of the design to make it slightly smaller than the front of the card.

4 Place the design behind the middle section of the card so that the stitching is in the centre of the opening.

5 Place the wadding (batting) on the back of the design.

6 Stick double-sided tape around the edges of the middle section. Remove the backing and gently fold over the card edge to seal the design within the card.

Making a bookmark

A popular way to present cross-stitch work is to make it into a bookmark. It's an easy idea which simply requires finishing and backing.

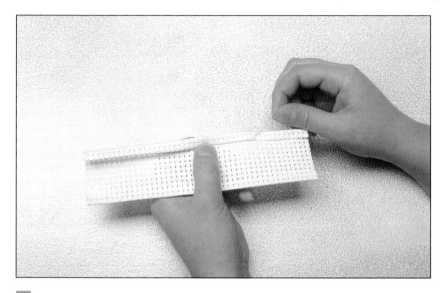

1 Turn a small seam on both of the long sides of your work and stitch using a backstitch to secure them.

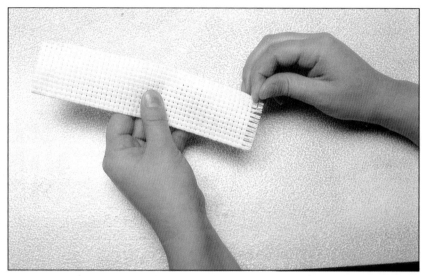

2 Using a needle or pin, pull away 1 cm (½ in) of threads at the top and bottom of the bookmark to make a fringe.

3 Cut a piece of felt very slightly smaller than the size of your bookmark.

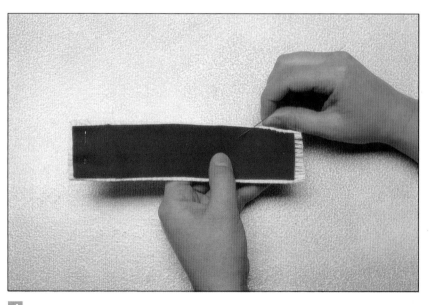

4 Oversew the piece of felt to the back of your work, enclosing the underside of the design and leaving you with a neat finish.

Violet glasses case

Dainty violets are an ideal motif for a practical
spectacles case. Keep your glasses safe and clean
in this attractive handbag-size case.

YOU WILL NEED

Design size: 23 x 27
fabric: 28 hpi evenweave over two
    threads, two pieces, 12 x 20 cm
    (4³⁄₄ x 8 in) and 12 x 28 cm
    (4³⁄₄ x 11 in)
26 tapestry needle
stranded cotton, as listed in key
tape measure
iron
interfacing
pins
sharp needle
sewing thread
lining fabric, two pieces,
    11 x 28 cm (4¹⁄₄ x 11 in)
scissors
3 mm (¹⁄₈ in) satin ribbon
small button

stranded cotton

tape measure

sewing thread

sharp needle

fabric

26 tapestry needle

scissors

lining fabric

button

satin ribbon

interfacing

pins

MAKING-UP INSTRUCTIONS

1 First work the design on both pieces
of fabric, using two strands for cross
stitch and French knots, and one strand
for backstitch. The bottom stitch of the
motif should be approximately 4 cm
(1¹⁄₂ in) from the lower edge of the
smaller piece of fabric and approximately
3 cm (1¹⁄₄ in) from the lower edge of the
larger piece. Iron interfacing to the back
of both pieces of embroidery. With right
sides facing, pin, then tack (baste) a piece
of lining to the larger piece around three
edges, then machine stitch.

2 Turn right side out. Fold a short
piece of satin ribbon to make a loop and
position it in the centre of the remaining
short edge. Slip stitch this edge, enclosing
the ribbon.

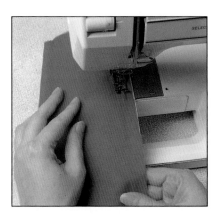

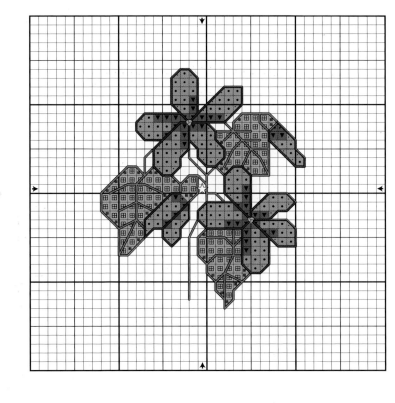

Cross stitch in two strands
97 Light violet
99 Mid violet
265 Very light hunter green

French knot in two strands
298 Orange

Backstitch in one strand
101 Dark violet
268 Dark hunter green

☆   Middle point

3 Repeat with the smaller piece of evenweave and lining, omitting the ribbon. Turn both pieces right side out and press.

4 Place the two pieces right sides together and stitch around the sides and lower edge, taking minimal turnings on sides. Stitch the button in place to close.

Apple-blossom coffee pot cover

Combine the evocative aromas of apple-blossom and coffee with this practical and charming coffee pot cover.

YOU WILL NEED
Design size: 147 x 91
fabric: 28 hpi evenweave over two
    threads, 30 x 20 cm (12 x 8 in)
26 tapestry needle
stranded cotton, as listed in key
iron
interfacing
2 pieces evenweave, 3 x 5 cm
    (1¼ x 2 in)
wadding (batting)
lining fabric
sharp needle
sewing thread
velcro
tape measure
pins
scissors

fabric

tape measure *26 tapestry needle*

stranded cotton

needle

lining fabric *wadding (batting)*

interfacing

sewing thread

scissors *pins*

velcro

MAKING-UP INSTRUCTIONS

1 Work your design using two strands for cross stitch and one strand for all backstitch. Iron interfacing to reverse of piece. Fold two small pieces of evenweave in half lengthwise and stitch the two long edges to make the flaps. Turn right side out and press.

2 Place embroidered piece, wadding (batting) and lining, right sides together, enclosing small pieces of evenweave on each short side. Stitch around three sides, leaving the bottom open. Turn right side out and press.

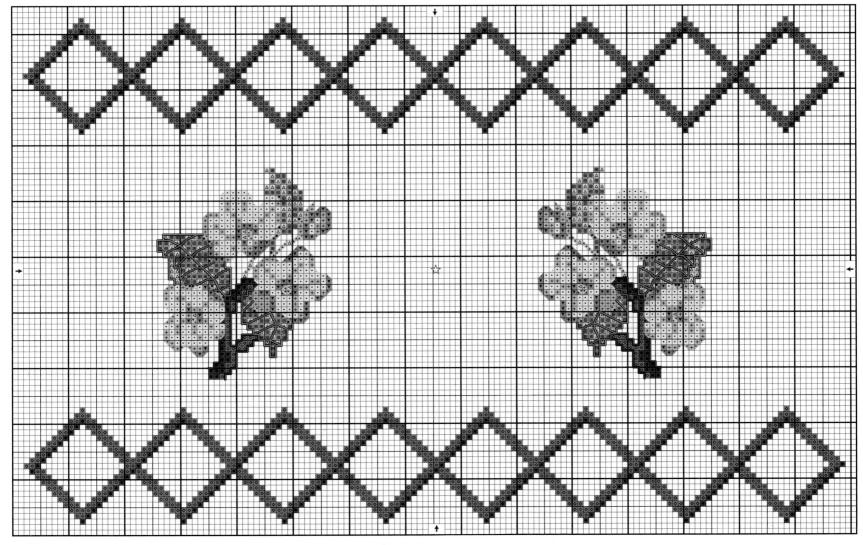

3 Sew one piece of velcro to each flap.

4 Stitch up remaining bottom edge.

Cross stitch in two strands

⊞ ⊞	242 Mid green
▼ ▼	26 Dark pink
◁ ◁	291 Yellow
● ●	370 Mid mink
• •	271 Light pink
+ +	73 Pale pink
△ △	240 Light grass green
◇ ◇	369 Mid rust

Backstitch in one strand

—	879 Very dark forest green
—	78 Very dark pink
—	359 Dark brown

☆   Middle point

Trout print

Moving slowly along the river, drifting through the gentle current, the smooth movement of the trout provides a tranquil respite from the hurried rush of everyday life.

YOU WILL NEED

Design size: 73 x 87
fabric: 28 hpi evenweave over two
    threads, 25 x 30 cm (10 x 12 in)
26 tapestry needle
stranded cotton, as listed in key
iron
towel
picture frame
ruler
pencil
cardboard
wadding (batting)
scissors
pins
sharp needle
sewing thread

Cross stitch in two strands

⊞ ⊞	168 Dark blue
S S	213 Very light leaf green
⊠ ⊠	215 Light leaf green
● ●	235 Mid grey
■ ■	236 Dark grey
↓ ↓	361 Light brown
✳ ✳	363 Dark brown
▽ ▽	858 Mint green
· ·	928 Light blue
⊒ ⊒	6 Light salmon
▼ ▼	9 Dark salmon
◇ ◇	234 Light grey

Backstitch in one strand

—   236 Dark grey

French knot in two strands

⊘   361 Light brown

☆   Middle point

stranded cotton

ruler

sewing thread

26 tapestry needle

pins

cardboard

fabric

scissors

wadding (batting)

pencil

sharp needle

1 Work the design using two strands for cross stitch and one for backstitch.

2 When the work is complete, check it for marks. If it is grubby, you can rinse the stitching in warm, soapy water.

3 Allow it to dry flat and press lightly with the stitching face down on a towel so that you don't flatten the stitches.

4 Mount your work by following the instructions for lacing a picture.

Otter pot

Look for the otter basking at the river's edge; it is a sure sign that spring has returned.

YOU WILL NEED
Design size: 33 x 32
fabric: 18 hpi Aida,
    10 x 10 cm (4 x 4 in)
26 tapestry needle
stranded cotton, as listed in key
iron
towel
7 cm (2½ in) craft pot
pencil
scissors
wadding (batting)

1 Starting from the centre of the design, work the otter using one strand throughout.

2 When the work is complete, check it for marks. If it is grubby, you can rinse the stitching in warm, soapy water.

3 Allow it to dry flat and press lightly with the stitching face down on a towel so that you don't flatten the stitches.

4 Mount your work by following the instructions for filling a pot.

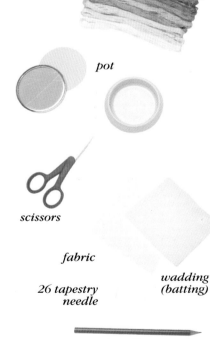

stranded cotton

pot

scissors

fabric

wadding (batting)

26 tapestry needle

pencil

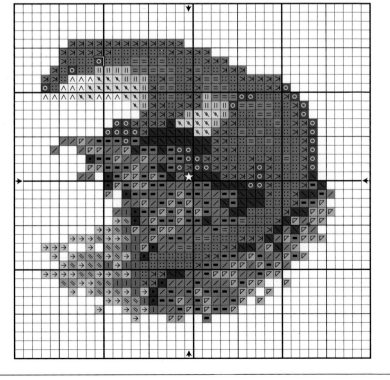

Cross stitch in one strand

I I	878 Dark forest green
• •	382 Very dark brown
⌐⌐	876 Mid forest green
→ →	875 Light forest green
▽ ▽	843 Dark green
∕ ∕	845 Sage
▬ ▬	681 Dark grey brown
◥	846 Brown
∧ ∧	926 Mid cream
⊠ ⊠	390 Deep cream
II II	391 Mushroom
= =	392 Dark mushroom
∴∴	903 Mid mushroom brown
⊳I	393 Very dark mushroom
o o	905 Mink brown

— Backstitch in one strand
391 mushroom

☆ Middle point

Duckling school gym bag

Pack your child off to school with a new and personal gym bag with their clean kit tucked inside. It's easy to make and any child will be proud to use it.

YOU WILL NEED
Design size: 117 x 120
fabric: 14 hpi Aida, 32 x 36 cm
  (13 x 14 in)
26 tapestry needle
stranded cotton, as listed in key
backing fabric
pins
sharp needle
sewing thread
scissors
tape measure
cord

stranded cotton

tape measure

sewing thread

scissors

cord

pins

fabric

26 tapestry needle

sharp needle

MAKING-UP INSTRUCTIONS

1 First work the design using two strands for cross stitch and one strand for backstitch. With right sides facing, pin and tack (baste) the embroidered piece to the backing fabric along the bottom and side edges.

2 Sew along the bottom and the two long sides, leaving a 4 cm (1½ in) gap at the top of one long edge. Turn the top edge under 2 cm (¾ in) and stitch close to the raw edge. Turn the bag to the right side.

Cross stitch in two strands

□ □	1 White
• •	137 Wedgwood blue
▨	906 Dark brown
→ →	368 Mid beige
– –	261 Mid grass green
I I	262 Dark grass green
■	403 Black
= =	302 Mid orange-yellow
⁖⁖	304 Orange
⊠ ⊠	288 Very pale yellow
◇ ◇	290 Pale yellow
◹ ◹	298 Deep yellow
▽ ▽	297 Mid yellow

Backstitch in one strand

—	403 Black

☆	Middle point

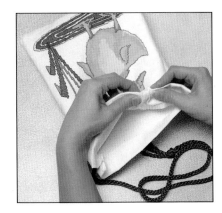

3 Thread the cord through the casing at the top of the bag. Finish by tying the ends of the cord in a knot.

TIP

When you spend a lot of time cross stitching you may find that your arm and shoulder feel stiff. Work with a light shining over your shoulder; the heat from the lamp will keep your muscles warm. Remember to stretch out your muscles every half-hour to keep them supple.

Bluebells cushion

Brighten up your sofa with this unique cushion decorated with a repeat design of bluebells.

Cross stitch in two strands

268 Dark hunter green		118 Mid blue	
267 Mid hunter green		109 Light blue	
266 Light hunter green		117 Very light blue	
265 Very light hunter green		297 Buttercup yellow	
119 Very dark blue			
111 Dark blue		☆ Middle point	

YOU WILL NEED

Design size: 142 x 142
fabric: 14 hpi Aida, 30 x 30 cm (12 x 12 in)
26 tapestry needle
stranded cotton, as listed in key
backing fabric
tape measure
scissors
pins
sewing thread
sharp needle
30 cm (12 in) zip (zipper)
28 cm (11 in) cushion pad

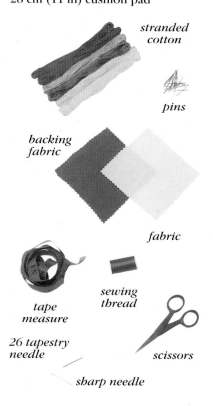

stranded cotton

pins

backing fabric

fabric

tape measure

sewing thread

26 tapestry needle

scissors

sharp needle

zip (zipper)

MAKING-UP INSTRUCTIONS

1 First work the design using two strands throughout. Lay the backing fabric over the embroidered piece with right sides facing. Stitch 1 cm (½ in) at either end of the top edge.

2 Insert the zip (zipper). With right sides facing, place the zip (zipper) behind the fabric. Tack (baste) and stitch the zip (zipper) to the edge of the backing fabric. Then tack (baste) and stitch the front piece to the zip (zipper).

3 Open the zip (zipper) slightly. With right sides facing, stitch around the three open sides. Clip the corners.

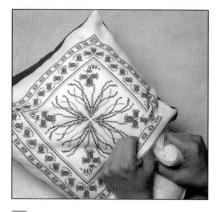

4 Unzip the cushion cover and turn it to the right side. Fill the cushion with the cushion pad.

Daisy shelf border

Repeat this reversed design to make a length of
original shelf border. You could use it along
kitchen or bedroom shelves or inside cupboards.

YOU WILL NEED
Design size: 22 x 128 repeat design
fabric: 14 hpi Aida band, 5 cm (2 in)
    wide band
26 tapestry needle
stranded cotton, as listed in key
sharp needle
sewing thread
scissors

stranded cotton

scissors *fabric*

*26 tapestry
needle*

sewing thread *sharp needle*

1 Working from the middle of the
piece of Aida band, stitch the design in
two strands for cross stitch and one
strand for backstitch.

2 When you have worked one motif,
start the next. The repeat motif begins
10 stitches into the previous one, so that
the leaves overlap.

3 When you have finished the border,
turn under each of the narrow edges
and slip stitch in place.

Cross stitch in two strands
| | | 1 White
| • • | 298 Mid yellow
| □□ | 227 Mid green

Backstitch in one strand
—— 403 Black

☆ Middle point

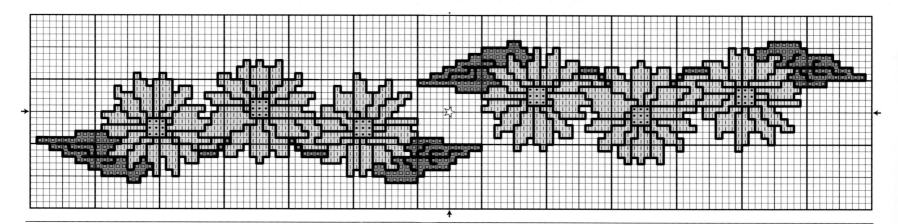

Swallows pot

Trinket boxes are always popular. This delicate swallow design is ideal for decorating a box to sit on your dressing-table.

YOU WILL NEED
Design size: 35 x 36
fabric: 18 hpi Aida, 10 x 10 cm
   (4 x 4 in)
26 tapestry needle
stranded cotton, as listed in key
iron
towel
7 cm (2½ in) craft pot
wadding (batting)
pencil
scissors

1 Starting from the centre of the design, work the cross stitch using one strand throughout.

2 When the work is complete, check for marks. If it is grubby, you can rinse the stitching in warm, soapy water.

3 Allow it to dry flat and press lightly with the stitching face down on a towel so that you don't flatten the stitches.

4 Mount your work by following the instructions for filling a pot.

stranded cotton

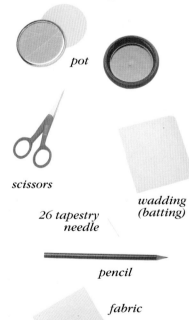

pot

scissors

26 tapestry needle

wadding (batting)

pencil

fabric

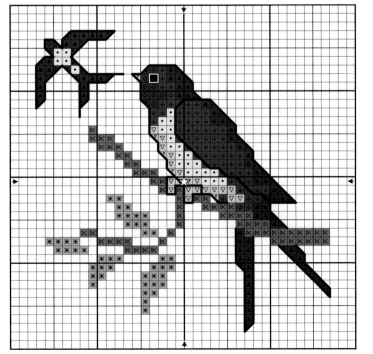

Cross stitch in one strand

▽ ▽	886 Dark cream
• •	926 Mid cream
⊠ ⊠	349 Brown
■	403 Black
◇ ◗	1006 Red
▲ ▲	150 Dark blue
✳ ✳	226 Green
▼ ↓	148 Blue

Backstitch in one strand

——	403 Black
=	2 White
☆	Middle point

Primrose picture frame

If you are looking for an interesting frame, why not create your own with this attractive design?

YOU WILL NEED

Design size: 93 x 117
fabric: 28 hpi natural evenweave
   over two threads, 25 x 20 cm
   (10 x 8 in)
26 tapestry needle
stranded cotton, as listed in key
cardboard mount and backing
   board (pre-cut to size)
ruler
pencil
scissors
double-sided tape or glue
wadding (batting)
   (pre-cut to size)

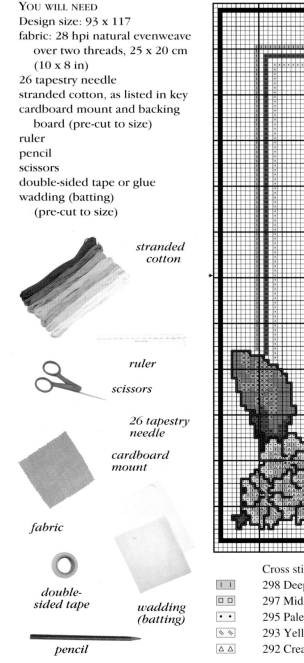

stranded cotton

ruler

scissors

26 tapestry needle

cardboard mount

fabric

double-sided tape

wadding (batting)

pencil

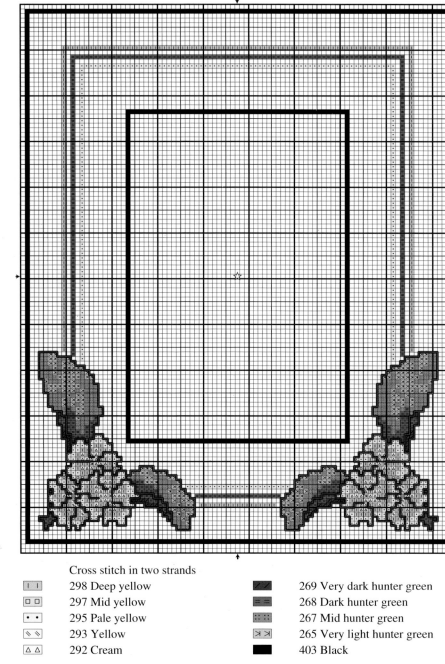

1 First stitch the design using two strands for cross stitch and one strand for backstitch. Place your pre-cut cardboard mount centrally over the design. Using a ruler and pencil, draw a cross from corner to corner of the aperture (opening).

2 Cut along the lines of the cross, taking care to cut into the corners. Cut out the middle section, leaving a 2 cm (³/₄ in) allowance. Position the pre-cut wadding (batting) and backing board on the back of the design.

Cross stitch in two strands

I I	298 Deep yellow
□ □	297 Mid yellow
• •	295 Pale yellow
◊ ◊	293 Yellow
△ △	292 Cream

∕∕	269 Very dark hunter green
= =	268 Dark hunter green
⋮⋮	267 Mid hunter green
⊳ ⊳	265 Very light hunter green
■	403 Black

Backstitch in one strand

—	269 Very dark hunter green
—	905 Mink brown
☆	Middle point

32

3 Cut the edges of the fabric to within 2 cm (³/₄ in) of the mount board. Using double-sided tape, fold and stick the edges to the back of the board. Use double-sided tape to fix a piece of card to the back of the frame.

4 To finish, glue a cardboard stand to the back. If you prefer, you could use double-sided tape to fix the stand in place.

Kingfisher shopping bag

Make yourself a colourful shopping bag covered in iridescent kingfishers. They sit in anticipation on a branch, waiting for food.

YOU WILL NEED

Design size: 158 x 66
fabric: 14 hpi Aida,
    46 x 15 cm (18 x 6 in)
26 tapestry needle
stranded cotton, as listed in key
Kreinik blending filaments, as listed
    in key
scissors
canvas fabric
calico lining fabric
tape measure
sharp needle
sewing thread
pins
iron

sewing thread

pins

stranded cotton

Kreinik blending filaments

scissors

sharp needle

tape measure

26 tapestry needle *canvas fabric*

fabric

calico lining

MAKING-UP INSTRUCTIONS

1 First work the design using two strands throughout. Cut two 46 x 41 cm (18 x 16 in) pieces of the canvas fabric and the calico lining for the bag. Cut two 10 x 43 cm (4 x 17 in) strips of canvas fabric for handles. Turn under the long edges of the embroidered fabric by 1 cm (½ in). Tack (baste) and stitch on to the front piece of the bag.

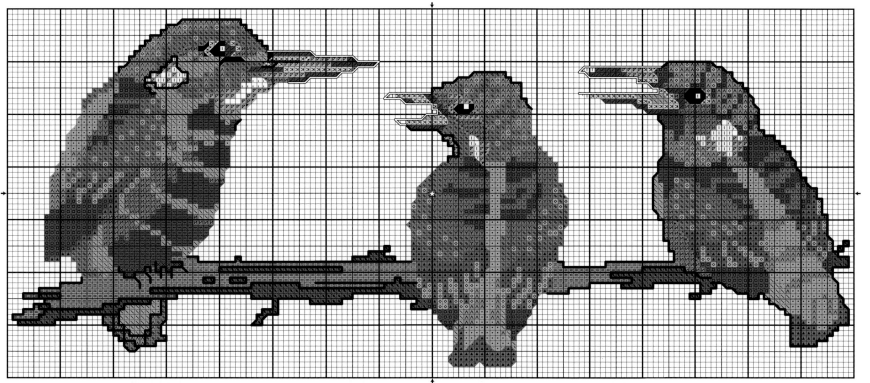

2 With right sides facing, pin the canvas bag front and back together. Machine stitch along the sides and the bottom edge with a 1 cm (¹/₂ in) seam. Press the seam. Stitch the lining sections together, but do not turn right side out.

3 To make the handles, fold each smaller canvas piece in half lengthwise with right sides facing. Machine stitch the long side, turn right side out and press. Position one handle on the front of the bag with the raw edges of the handle matching the raw top edge of the bag. Position the second handle on the back of the bag. Fold the handles against the body of the bag.

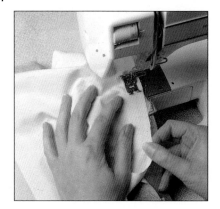

4 With right sides facing, insert the lining. Stitch the lining to the body, enclosing the handles with a 1 cm (¹/₂ in) seam. Leave a gap for turning. Pull the bag through the gap and pin, then tack (baste) and slip stitch the gap. Press the bag to finish.

Cross stitch in two strands

1 White	
167	Light turquoise
169	Mid turquoise
170	Dark turquoise
326	Rusty orange
349	Caramel
379	Mid beige
403	Black
858	Green grey
875	Light forest green
889	Dark brown
900	Pearl grey
1041	Dark slate grey
1047	Light peach
1048	Mid peach
167/169	Blend light/mid turquoise
877/779	Blend sea green/slate blue
779	Slate blue/Kreinik sky blue HL

Backstitch in two strands

— 1 White
— 403 Black

☆ Middle point

Fledglings picture

The sound of fledglings chirping from their nest, waiting for their parents to bring them food, is a sure sign of spring.

1 Work the design using two strands for cross stitch and one or two strands for backstitch as indicated in the key.

2 When the work is complete, check it for marks. If it is grubby, you can rinse the stitching in warm, soapy water.

3 Allow it to dry flat and press lightly with the stitching face down on a towel so that you don't flatten the stitches.

4 Mount your work by following the instructions for lacing a picture.

YOU WILL NEED
Design size: 83 x 118
fabric: 14 hpi Aida, 23 x 28 cm
    (9 x 11 in)
26 tapestry needle
stranded cotton, as listed in key
iron
towel
ruler
pencil
cardboard
wadding (batting)
scissors
pins
sharp needle
sewing thread
picture frame

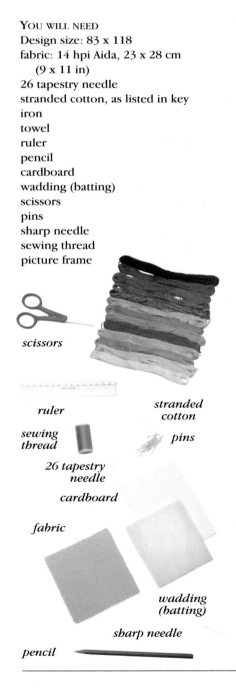

scissors

ruler

sewing thread

stranded cotton

pins

26 tapestry needle

cardboard

fabric

wadding (batting)

sharp needle

pencil

Cross stitch in two strands

			73 Pale pink
		77 Cerise pink
		241 Light green
		243 Mid green
		(in bird's beak)
		245 Dark green
|| ||	275 Ecru
		304 Orange
		306 Mid gold
		355 Mid cranberry
		357 Dark cranberry
		369 Mid rust
		376 Light beige
		379 Mid beige
		403 Black
		830 Light taupe
		831 Mid taupe
		855 Dark khaki
		856 Mid khaki
		874 Bright yellow
		889 Dark brown
		898 Mid brown
+ +	907 Yolk yellow
		1045 Deep yolk yellow

Cross stitch in mixed strands
(one of each colour)

1045/355 Deep yolk yellow/
mid cranberry

855/853 Dark khaki/light khaki

Backstitch in one strand

357 Dark cranberry

77 Cerise pink

403 Black (beaks)

Backstitch in two strands

898 Mid brown

856 Mid khaki

369 Mid rust (border)

355 Mid cranberry (border)

357 Dark cranberry (border)

275 Ecru (small stitch in eyes)

☆   Middle point

Aconites sampler

The instantly recognizable yellows of the aconites
bring a touch of cheer to a wintry landscape.

YOU WILL NEED
Design size: 85 x 85
fabric: 28 hpi evenweave over two
    threads, 25 x 25 cm (10 x 10 in)
26 tapestry needle
stranded cotton, as listed in key
iron
towel
ruler
pencil
cardboard
wadding (batting)
scissors
pins
sharp needle
sewing thread
picture frame

stranded cotton

scissors

ruler

pins

26 tapestry needle

cardboard

wadding (batting)

fabric

sewing thread

sharp needle

pencil

Cross stitch in two strands

110 Dark lilac
167 Light turquoise
168 Dark turquoise
205 Dark blue-green
206 Light blue-green
238 Bright green
253 Light yellow-green
254 Mid green
288 Very pale yellow
298 Deep yellow
311 Light orange
314 Dark orange
358 Dark mink
399 Grey
295 Pale yellow
13 Red
90 Light lilac

Backstitch in one strand
358 Dark mink

French knot in one strand
403 Black

☆ Middle point

1 Work the design using two strands for cross stitch and one strand for backstitch and French knots.

2 When the work is complete, check it for marks. If it is grubby, you can rinse the stitching in warm, soapy water to remove any marks.

3 Allow it to dry flat and press lightly with the stitching face down on a towel so that you don't flatten the stitches.

4 Mount your work by following the instructions for lacing a picture.

Rainbow bookmark

Save your page with this striking array of rainbow colours. A bookmark is both useful and attractive and it is an easy project for the cross stitcher.

YOU WILL NEED
Design size: 87 x 30
fabric: 18 hpi Aida, 20 x 7.5 cm
 (8 x 3 in)
26 tapestry needle
stranded cotton, as listed in key
iron
scissors
sewing thread
sharp needle
felt
pins

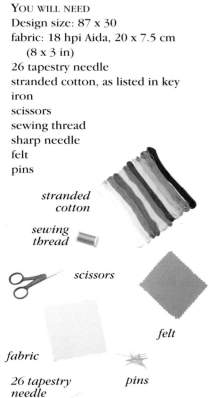

stranded cotton

sewing thread

scissors

felt

fabric

26 tapestry needle

pins

needle

1 Work the design using two strands for all the cross stitch except the rainbow, which uses two strands for the bottom stitch and one strand for the top stitch. Work all the backstitch in one strand. Press the long edges of the embroidered piece to the wrong side and trim to within four squares of the fold line.

2 Using small neat stitches, hand sew a strip of felt on to the back of the embroidery, ensuring it is equidistant from both ends.

3 Machine stitch through the Aida and the felt, seven squares from each short edge of the embroidery.

4 Trim the Aida 10 squares away from the machine-stitched line. Next, remove the threads along the short edges of the bookmark to six squares deep to make a fringe.

Cross stitch in two strands for lower stitch and one strand of 928 for top stitch

1006 Red		238 Bright green
314 Orange		142 Dark blue
291 Yellow		101 Dark violet

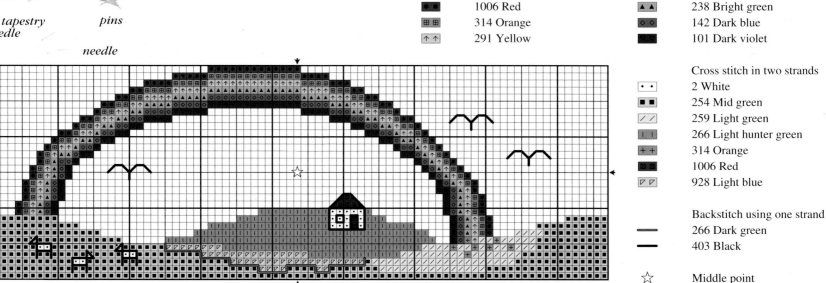

Cross stitch in two strands
2 White
254 Mid green
259 Light green
266 Light hunter green
314 Orange
1006 Red
928 Light blue

Backstitch using one strand
— 266 Dark green
— 403 Black

☆ Middle point

Ladybird paperweight

You could use this paperweight to keep your kitchen notes and recipes tidy. The ladybird is a versatile motif; use the design to decorate a shelf border and coordinate the room.

YOU WILL NEED
Design size: 32 x 33
fabric: 14 hpi Aida, 13 x 13 cm
   (5 x 5 in)
26 tapestry needle
stranded cotton, as listed in key
8 cm (3 in) craft paperweight
pencil
scissors

1 First work the design using two strands for cross stitch and one strand for backstitch.

2 When complete, draw around the piece of felt supplied with the paperweight on to your design. Ensure the motif is centred.

3 Cut neatly around the drawn line on the embroidered piece.

4 Place the embroidery under the weight with the design facing into the glass and finish by placing the sticky felt on the bottom.

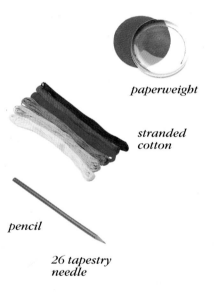

paperweight

stranded cotton

pencil

26 tapestry needle

scissors   *fabric*

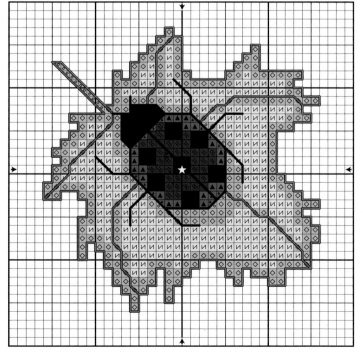

Cross stitch in two strands
и и   259 Light green
◇ ◇   265 Very light hunter green
▲ ▲   335 Light red
■   403 Black
▨   9046 Dark red

Backstitch in one strand
───   268 Dark hunter green
───   403 Black

☆   Middle point

Bees padded coat hanger

Covered coat hangers help to stop delicate garments being snagged and pulled out of shape. This busy bees design makes an elegant hanger.

YOU WILL NEED

Design size: 215 x 41
fabric: 28 hpi evenweave over two
    threads, 50 x 15 cm (20 x 6 in)
26 tapestry needle
stranded cotton, as listed in key
pencil
scissors
backing fabric
wadding (batting)
pins
120 cm (48 in) of 1 cm (½ in) lace
sharp needle
sewing thread
coat hanger
6 mm (¼ in) satin ribbon
double-sided tape

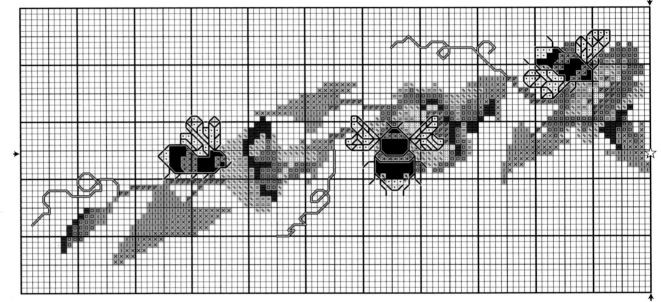

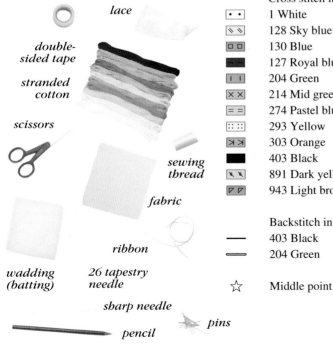

lace
double-sided tape
stranded cotton
scissors
sewing thread
fabric
ribbon
wadding (batting)
26 tapestry needle
sharp needle
pencil
pins

Cross stitch in two strands

· ·	1 White
◆ ◆	128 Sky blue
□ □	130 Blue
■ ■	127 Royal blue
I I	204 Green
× ×	214 Mid green
= =	274 Pastel blue
⸬ ⸬	293 Yellow
▷ ▷	303 Orange
■	403 Black
⊠ ⊠	891 Dark yellow
▽ ▽	943 Light brown

Backstitch in one strand

——	403 Black
══	204 Green
☆	Middle point

MAKING-UP INSTRUCTIONS

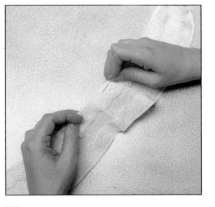

1 First work the design, reversing the pattern to make the second half. Make a template from the hanger and use this as a guide to cut hanger shapes from the embroidered fabric, the backing fabric and two pieces of wadding (batting).

2 Pin the length of lace to the backing fabric with right sides facing and raw edges matching. Gather the lace a little around the corners if necessary. Tack (baste) and sew.

3 With right sides facing, place the embroidered fabric on top of the laced backing fabric. Lay a piece of wadding (batting) on each side and tack (baste) into position. Stitch around the lower edge and curves, leaving the top edge open. Trim the wadding (batting), clip the corners and turn to the right side.

4 Bind the hanger hook with ribbon by applying a piece of double-sided tape to the top of the hook. Work ribbon over this and tape the opposite end of the ribbon to the hanger. Insert the hanger into the cover, turn under the raw edges and close the top edges by slip stitching them together.

Heron card

Inspired by an original watercolour, this special greetings card has been designed for you to stitch and give to a deserving friend.

YOU WILL NEED
Design size: 60 x 97
fabric: 18 hpi Aida, 12 x 17 cm
  (4½ x 6½ in)
26 tapestry needle
stranded cotton, as listed in key
iron
towel
card with opening
pencil
wadding (batting)
scissors
double-sided tape

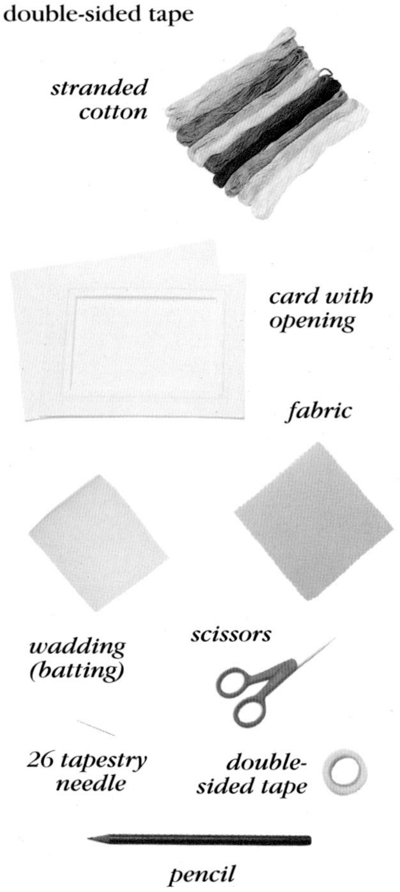

stranded cotton

card with opening

fabric

wadding (batting)

scissors

26 tapestry needle

double-sided tape

pencil

1 Starting from the centre of the design, work the heron using one strand throughout.

2 When the work is complete, check it for marks. If it is grubby, you can rinse the stitching in warm, soapy water.

3 Allow it to dry flat and press lightly with the stitching face down on a towel so that you don't flatten the stitches.

4 Mount your work by following the instructions for filling a card.

Cross stitch in one strand

	1 White	
	403 Black	
	218 Dark green	
	214 Mid green	
	266 Hunter green	
	381 Dark brown	
	295 Pale yellow	
	891 Dark yellow	
	235 Dark grey	
	234 Light grey	
	399 Mid grey	
	274 Pastel blue	
	850 Mid grey-blue	

Backstitch in one strand

236 Very dark grey
403 Black
399 Mid grey
891 Dark yellow
381 Dark brown

French knot in one strand

● 236 Very dark grey

☆ Middle point

Rabbit coaster

Wildlife subjects are always popular and the rabbit is a particular favourite. You're sure to get a smile from friends when you present them with a set of these charming coasters.

YOU WILL NEED
Design size: 37 x 32
fabric: 18 hpi Aida, 10 x 10 cm
   (4 x 4 in)
26 tapestry needle
stranded cotton, as listed in key
8 cm (3 in) craft coaster
pencil
scissors

1 First work the design using one strand throughout.

2 When complete, draw around the piece of felt supplied with the coaster on to your design, centring the motif under the felt.

3 Cut neatly around the drawn line on the design.

4 Place the embroidery face upwards in the coaster. Finish by placing the sticky felt on the back.

stranded cotton

scissors

26 tapestry needle

craft coaster

pencil

fabric

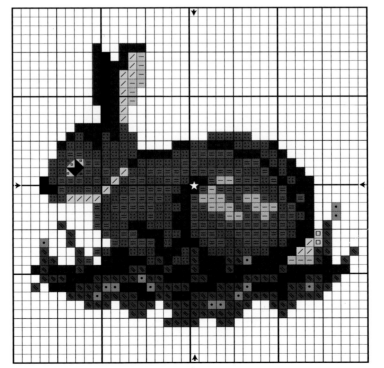

Cross stitch in one strand
269 Very dark hunter green
266 Hunter green
268 Dark hunter green
2 Ecru
368 Deep cream
276 Mid cream
370 Mid mink
358 Dark mink
380 Dark brown
382 Chocolate brown

☆ Middle point

Hedgehog pot

Even though a real hedgehog's back is covered in unwelcoming prickly spines, a sewn hedgehog always looks cute. Our cuddly hedgehog looks super mounted in the lid of a useful trinket pot.

YOU WILL NEED
Design size: 39 x 24
fabric: 18 hpi Aida, 10 x 10 cm
   (4 x 4 in)
26 tapestry needle
stranded cotton, as listed in key
iron
towel
7 cm (2¹/₂ in) craft pot
pencil
scissors
wadding (batting)

1 Starting from the centre of the design, work the hedgehog using two strands throughout.

2 When the work is complete, check it for marks. If it is grubby, you can rinse the stitching in warm, soapy water.

3 Allow it to dry flat and press lightly with the stitching face down on a towel so that you don't flatten the stitches.

4 Mount your work by following the instructions for filling a pot.

stranded cotton

pot

fabric

wadding (batting)

scissors

26 tapestry needle

pencil

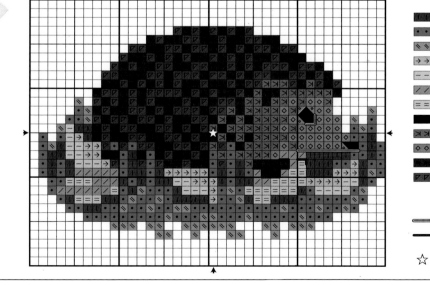

Cross stitch in two strands
269 Very dark hunter green
268 Dark hunter green
266 Hunter green
907 Sage green
874 Light sage green
365 Mid rust
363 Light tan
403 Black
379 Mid mink
400 Slate grey
382 Chocolate brown
236 Dark grey

Backstitch in two strands
403 Black
382 Chocolate brown

☆ Middle point

Peacock book cover

Capture the essence of the regal yet flamboyant peacock by decorating this original book cover with beads and blended threads.

YOU WILL NEED
Design size: 90 x 120
fabric: 14 hpi Aida, 36 x 90 cm
   (14 x 36 in)
sharp needle
sewing thread
24 tapestry needle
Kreinik thread, as listed in key
embroidery frame
glass beads
hardback book
tape measure
pencil
scissors
iron
small crochet hook

pencil

crochet hook

tape measure

hardback book

sewing thread

Kreinik thread

scissors

beads

sewing thread

fabric

embroidery frame

needle

MAKING-UP INSTRUCTIONS

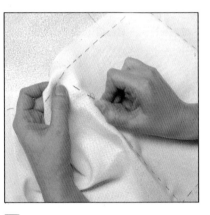

1 Mark up the fabric for stitching. Tack (baste) a line 20 cm (8 in) from the right-hand edge. Work the design using one strand of Kreinik thread throughout.

2 Measure the fabric needed for the book cover to include two pockets. Trim the excess fabric, leaving 4 cm (1½ in) for hems. Machine stitch the hems all round, turning under 2 cm (¾ in) twice. Clip the corners and oversew them.

3 Fold the fabric at the front edge to make a pocket and slip stitch along the top and bottom edges. Press the cover, then wrap it around the book. Fold the fabric into the back cover to make the back pocket. Slip stitch along the edges.

4 Make two 55 cm (21½ in) long cords by crocheting chains using three strands of Kreinik threads. Thread beads on to the ends of the chains, finish with a series of knots and attach to the top and bottom of the inside of the fabric cover.

Cross stitch in one strand
Kreinik fine braid (#8) - 002
Kreinik fine braid (#8) - 009
Kreinik fine braid (#8) - 005
Kreinik fine braid (#8) - 008
Kreinik fine braid (#8) - 008
+002

Backstitch in one strand
Kreinik fine braid (#8) - 005

Beading
Mill Hill glass seed
beads 62013

Cross stitch twice in the same holes
in one strand
Kreinik fine braid (#8) - 051

☆ Middle point

TIP

When adding beads to a design, use
a beading needle threaded with
sewing thread. Begin stitching as if
you were making a half cross stitch,
but before taking the needle back
through the fabric, push a single
bead through the needle and on to
the thread. Put the needle back
through the fabric to finish the half
cross stitch. Work the next stitch.

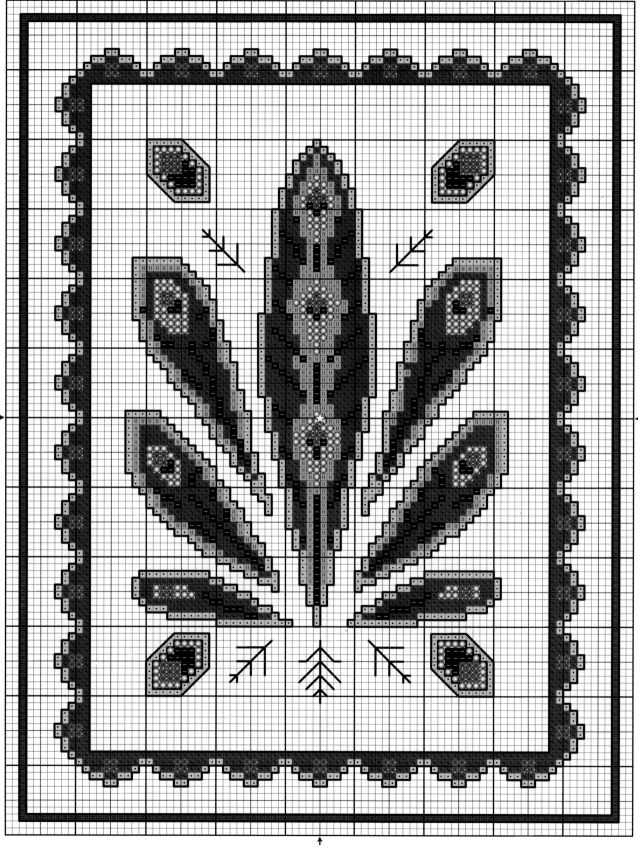

Frogs on waterlilies tray cloth

Create a tea-time treat and add a touch of humour to an afternoon snack with this whimsical tray cloth.

YOU WILL NEED
Design size: 118 x 80
fabric: 14 hpi Aida, two pieces,
    18 x 25 cm (7 x 10 in)
26 tapestry needle
stranded cotton, as listed in key
mini craft tray 18 x 25 cm (7 x 10 in)
scissors

1 Starting from the centre, work the design using two strands for cross stitch and one for backstitch and French knots.

2 Lift the insert out of the middle of the tray.

3 Cut a piece of backing fabric the same size as the embroidered piece.

4 Put the backing fabric into the tray, followed by the embroidery and, finally, the insert.

26 tapestry needle

scissors

stranded cotton

pencil

fabric

mini craft tray

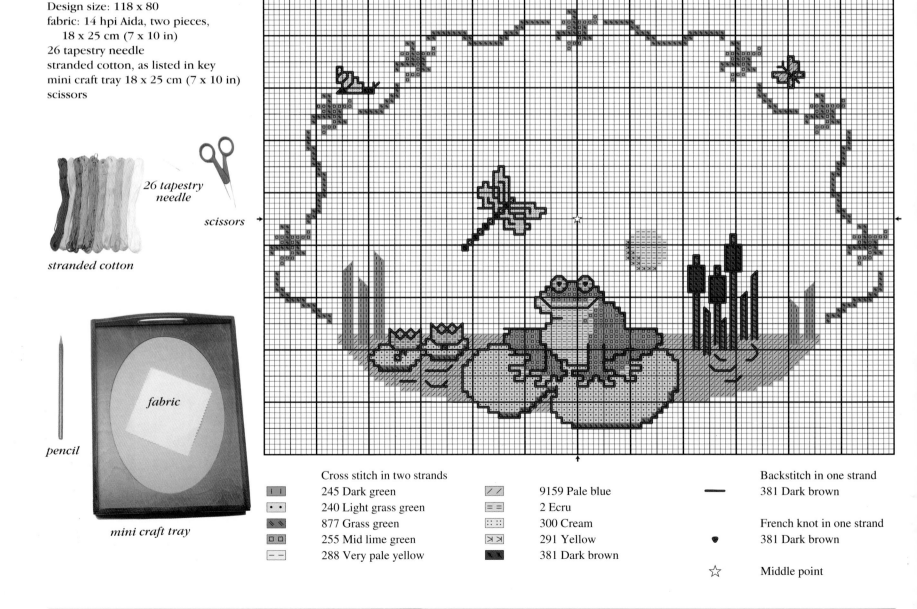

Cross stitch in two strands				Backstitch in one strand	
	245 Dark green		9159 Pale blue	—	381 Dark brown
	240 Light grass green		2 Ecru		
	877 Grass green		300 Cream		French knot in one strand
	255 Mid lime green		291 Yellow	●	381 Dark brown
	288 Very pale yellow		381 Dark brown		
				☆	Middle point

Golden pheasant cabinet

Making a regal stance in the centre of this elegant cabinet, the golden pheasant will take pride of place in your home.

YOU WILL NEED
Design size: 45 x 45
fabric: 28 hpi evenweave over two
    threads, 15 x 15 cm (6 x 6 in)
26 tapestry needle
stranded cotton, as listed in key
craft display cabinet
cardboard
pencil
scissors
wadding (batting)
double-sided tape

1 Starting from the centre, work the cross stitch in two strands and the backstitch in one or two strands.

2 Cut a piece of cardboard to fit the centre section of the cabinet.

3 Place the embroidered piece face down on a flat surface and cut a piece of wadding (batting) the same size. Centre it over the embroidery and place the cardboard on top.

4 Attach double-sided tape around the edges of the cardboard and fold the edges of the fabric over to fix them on to the tape. Position the embroidery in the centre section of the cabinet.

scissors

fabric

stranded cotton

double-sided tape

wadding (batting)

craft display cabinet

26 tapestry needle

pencil

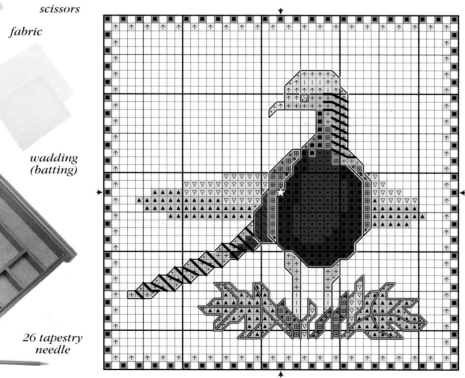

Cross stitch in two strands
▲ ▲	254 Dark yellow-green
◸ ◹	133 Blue
↑ ↑	305 Light gold
■ ■	308 Dark gold
██	403 Black
▬ ▬	1005 Dark red
I I	885 Cream
▽ ▽	259 Light green
▦ ▦	47 Light red
⊞ ⊞	227 Mid green
+ +	306 Mid gold

Backstitch in one strand
—	403 Black
—	268 Dark hunter green

Backstitch in two strands
—	403 Black

French knot in one strand
☺	885 Cream

☆	Middle point

Dragonfly card

The beautiful, iridescent colours of the dragonfly are dramatically brought to life on this atmospheric card.

You will need

Design size: 35 x 43
fabric: 14 hpi Aida, 9 x 12 cm
  (3½ x 4½ in)
26 tapestry needle
stranded cotton, as listed in key
iron
towel
card with opening
pencil
wadding (batting)
scissors
double-sided tape

1 Starting from the centre of the design, work the dragonfly using two strands for cross stitch and one strand for backstitch.

2 When you have completed the design, check it for any marks. If it is grubby, you can rinse the stitching in warm, soapy water.

3 Allow it to dry flat and press lightly with the stitching face down on a towel so that you don't flatten the stitches.

4 Mount your work by following the instructions for filling a card.

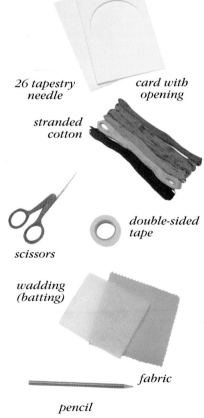

26 tapestry needle

card with opening

stranded cotton

double-sided tape

scissors

wadding (batting)

fabric

pencil

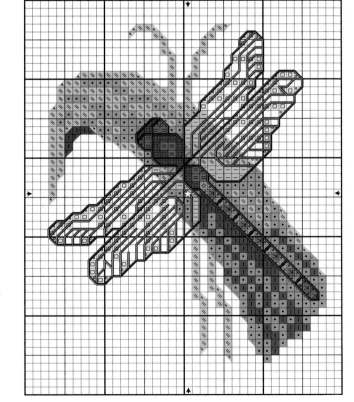

Cross stitch in two strands

	217 Dark leaf green
	216 Mid leaf green
	215 Light leaf green
	Kreinik 094
	Kreinik 094 and Anchor 215 (one strand of each)
	210 Light blue green
	923 Mid blue green
	212 Dark blue green
	164 Deep turquoise
	170 Mid turquoise

Backstitch in one strand

—	683 Dark green
—	152 Dark blue

☆ Middle point

Honeysuckle café curtain border design

This creeping design covers the bottom of a curtain with panache and style.

YOU WILL NEED
Design size: 120 x 50 repeat design
fabric: 14 hpi Aida band, 10 x 87 cm
   (4 x 34 in)
24 tapestry needle
Marlitt thread, as listed in key
embroidery frame (optional)
scissors
1 m (39 in) cotton fabric
tape measure
pins
sharp needle
sewing thread
iron

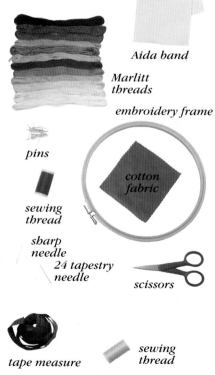

Aida band

Marlitt threads

embroidery frame

pins

cotton fabric

sewing thread

sharp needle

24 tapestry needle

scissors

tape measure

sewing thread

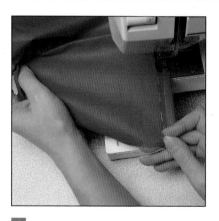

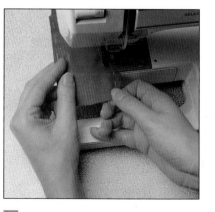

1 Work the design using two strands of Marlitt for cross stitch and one strand for backstitch and French knots. To make the curtain tabs, cut 16 pieces of cotton fabric, each one 10 x 26 cm (4 x 10 in). Position them in pairs with right sides facing. Pin, tack (baste) and machine stitch each pair together along three edges, leaving one short edge open. Turn right side out and press.

2 To make the curtain, turn under the side seams of the curtain by 2 cm (³/₄ in) twice and machine stitch.

3 Pin and tack (baste) a hem at the top and bottom of the curtain, then stitch the bottom hem. Fold the eight tabs in half and tack (baste) them in position evenly along the top edge of the curtain. Machine stitch the top hem, enclosing the tabs.

Cross stitch in two strands
Marlitt 895
Marlitt 1040
Marlitt 1039
Marlitt 894
Marlitt 881
Marlitt 852
Marlitt 897
Marlitt 1013
Marlitt 1212
Marlitt 893
Marlitt 1019

Backstitch in one strand
Marlitt 894
Marlitt 801

French knot in one strand
Marlitt 894

French knot in one strand
Marlitt 1072

☆ Middle point

4 Attach the embroidered border. Place it directly above the bottom hem. Turn under the edges on the narrower sides and machine stitch to the curtain.

Lavender hat band

Brighten up a summer hat with a simple cross-stitch design. You can complete this lavender hat band in an evening.

YOU WILL NEED

Design size: 40 x 21 repeat
fabric: 5 cm (2 in) wide, 14 hpi Aida
    band, 1 m (1⅛ yd)
26 tapestry needle
stranded cotton, as listed in key
hat
tape measure
pins
scissors
sharp needle
sewing thread
iron

hat

stranded cotton

sewing thread

scissors

Aida band

pins

needle

26 tapestry needle

tape measure

MAKING-UP INSTRUCTIONS

1 Starting from the centre of the band, work the design using two strands for cross stitch and one strand for backstitch. Measure around the hat.

2 Use this measurement to find the centre point of the Aida band and mark it with a pin. Cut the band to size, leaving 1 cm (½ in) at each end for a seam. With right sides facing, backstitch along the seam. Press the seam open.

3 Pull the band over the hat, making sure the seam sits at the back of the hat.

Cross stitch in two strands
▬ 112 Deep lavender
⣿ 98 Deep violet

Backstitch in one strand
— 263 Deep forest green

☆ Middle point

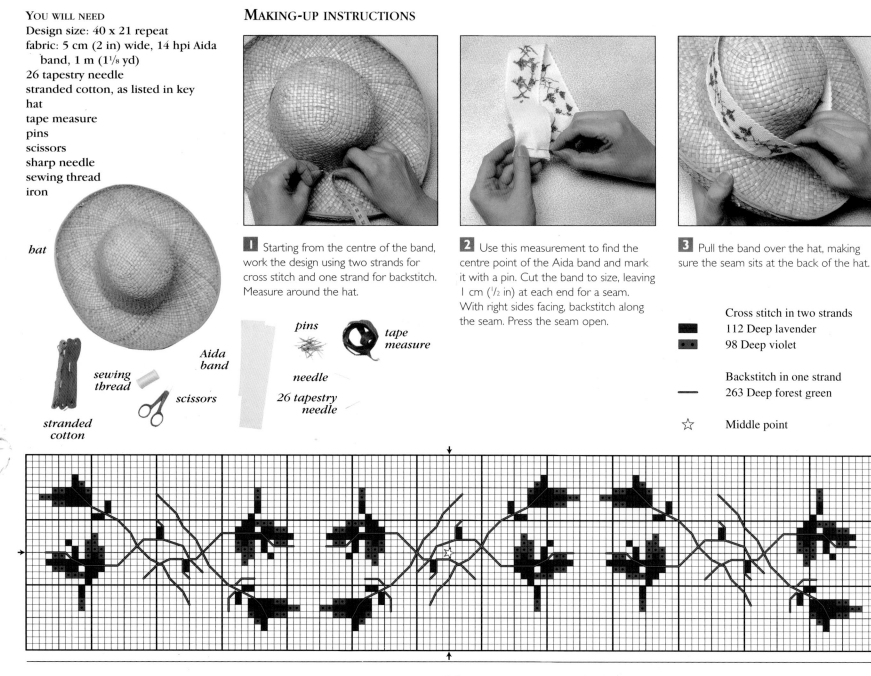

Corn-cob pot

Keep your Thanksgiving treats in this attractive harvest pot. And when you're done, use it to hold small change.

YOU WILL NEED

Design size: 42 x 36
fabric: 18 hpi Aida, 10 x 10 cm
　(4 x 4 in)
26 tapestry needle
stranded cotton, as listed in key
iron
towel
7 cm (2½ in) craft pot
pencil
scissors
wadding (batting)

1 Starting from the centre of the design, work the cross stitch using two strands throughout.

2 When the work is complete, check it for marks. If it is grubby, you can rinse the stitching in warm, soapy water.

3 Allow it to dry flat and press lightly with the stitching face down on a towel so that you don't flatten the stitches.

4 Mount your work by following the instructions for filling a pot.

pot

stranded cotton

wadding (batting)

scissors

fabric

26 tapestry needle

pencil

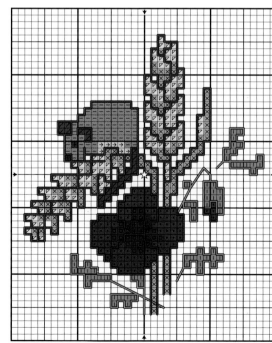

Cross stitch in two strands

▽ ▽	305 Light gold
■ ■	1006 Red
• •	46 Berry red
+ +	382 Chocolate brown
╱ ╱	351 Mid mink
→ →	367 Cream
– –	1048 Mid peach
I I	229 Mid forest green
✕ ✕	306 Mid gold

Backstitch in two strands

——	382 Chocolate brown
——	229 Mid forest green
☆	Middle point

Wild rose card

Delight your mother on Mother's Day with this pretty floral card.

YOU WILL NEED
Design size: 94 x 60
fabric: 18 hpi Aida, 15 x 18 cm
  (6 x 7 in)
26 tapestry needle
stranded cotton, as listed in key
iron
towel
card with opening
pencil
wadding (batting)
scissors
double-sided tape

1 Starting from the centre of the design, work the motif using one strand of thread throughout.

2 When the work is complete, check it for marks. If it is grubby, you can rinse the stitching in warm, soapy water.

3 Allow it to dry flat and press lightly with the stitching face down on a towel so that you don't flatten the stitches.

4 Mount your work by following the instructions for filling a card.

card with opening

stranded cotton

fabric

wadding (batting)

26 tapestry needle

double-sided tape

scissors

pencil

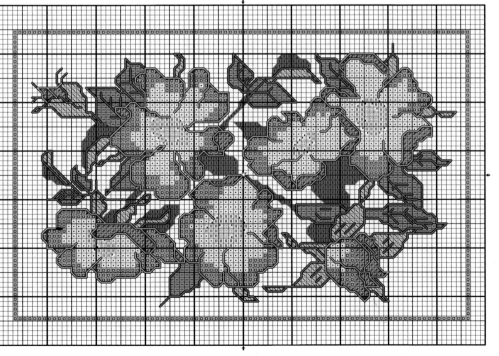

Cross stitch in one strand
271 Light pink
26 Dark pink
24 Mid pink
218 Dark green
216 Mid leaf green
214 Light leaf green
293 Yellow
278 Yellow-green

Backstitch in one strand
218 Dark green
54 Very dark pink

☆ Middle point

Butterfly shoulder-bag

Make yourself a unique shoulder-bag. This more challenging project uses beads, a variety of threads and a couple of different stitches.

MAKING-UP INSTRUCTIONS

1 Work the design using two strands of Marlitt thread for cross stitch and green French knots, and one strand for backstitch and black French knots. Use one strand of Kreinik throughout. Use sewing thread to attach the beads, working each stitch like a half cross stitch and threading on the bead before reinserting the thread into the fabric. Stitch the Aida and lining right sides together along the top and two sides.

YOU WILL NEED
Design size: 114 x 136
fabric: 14 hpi Aida, 30 x 71 cm
    (12 x 28 in)
24 tapestry needle
stranded cotton, as listed in key
Kreinik thread, as listed in key
Marlitt thread, as listed in key
embroidery frame
beading needle
small glass beads
cotton lining fabric, 1 m (39 in)
sewing thread
1 m (39 in) piping cord
sharp needle
7.5 cm (3 in) pieces of cardboard
pins
scissors
pencil

stranded cotton

scissors

needles

sewing thread
pencil

card-board

fabric

tape measure

piping cord

lining

beads

pins

Kreinik thread

embroidery frame

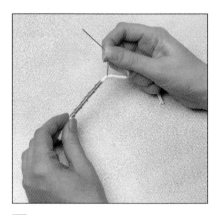

2 Make the bag strap by covering the piping cord with buttonhole stitch using four strands of Marlitt 858 and 863. Start buttonholing 2.5 cm (1 in) from the end of the cord.

3 Make the tassels by wrapping thread around a 7.5 cm (3 in) piece of card. Slide a length of thread under the cardboard and pull tightly, drawing the threads together. Remove the threads from the cardboard. Wrap a 75 cm (30 in) length around the threads and finish by stitching into the tassel.

4 Turn the bag to the right side and fold it in half. Turn under 2.5 cm (1 in) at the top edge. Insert the cord and hold it in place with a few stitches.

5 Pin, tack (baste) and oversew the edges of the bag together. Attach two tassels at either side of the bag top.

Cross stitch in one or two strands

	Marlitt 858 dark maroon
	Marlitt 863 maroon
	Kreinik fine braid 005 black
	Kreinik fine braid 001 light grey
	Marlitt 816 pearl grey
	Marlitt 817 light blue
	Marlitt 813 pale pink
	Marlitt 815 mid rose pink

	Marlitt 1069 dark rose pink
	Marlitt 853 green
	Marlitt 897 mint green
	Marlitt 852 blue green
	Marlitt 1072 brown
	Marlitt 859 purple
	Marlitt 857 light purple

Backstitch in one strand

— Marlitt 1072 brown
— Marlitt 801 black

Beading

● Mill Hill glass seed beads 00081

French knot in one strand

♥ Marlitt 801 black

French knot in one strand

❀ Marlitt 897 mint green

☆ Middle point

Oak tree hanging

The mighty oak is an emblem of constancy – strong and eternal. Create a symbolic hanging using this powerful subject.

YOU WILL NEED

Design size: 80 x 77
fabric: 28 hpi evenweave over two
    threads, 19 x 19 cm (7½ x 7½ in)
26 tapestry needle
stranded cotton, as listed in key
interfacing
iron
scissors
4 felt pieces, each 7.5 x 2.5 cm
    (3 x 1 in)
sharp needle
felt, 19 x 19 cm (7½ x 7½ in)
sewing thread
2 sticks, each 20 cm (8 in) long
cord with 2 tassels

tape measure

sticks

cord with tassels

pins

interfacing

stranded cotton

felt

scissors

fabric

sewing thread

needle

26 tapestry needle

	Cross stitch in two strands		Backstitch in one strand
■ ■	843 Dark green	—	236 Grey
⊞ ⊞	265 Very light hunter green	—	268 Dark hunter green
+ +	349 Brown		
▼ ▼	370 Mid mink	☆	Middle point
· ·	842 Light green		

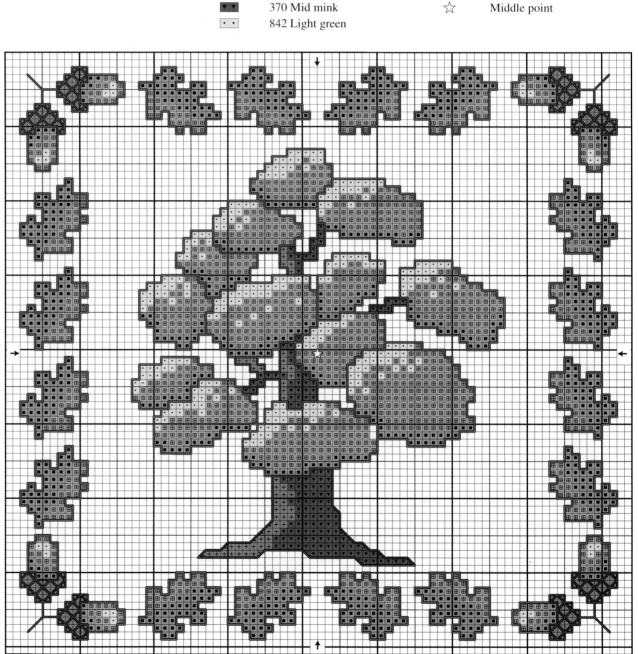

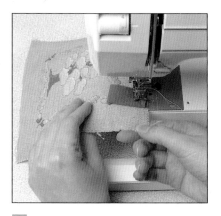

1 Starting from the centre of the design, work the motif using two strands for cross stitch and one strand for backstitch. Iron interfacing to the wrong side of the embroidered piece. Fold the pieces of felt in half across their width. Tack (baste) two felt tabs to the top of the embroidered piece and two to the bottom, approximately 2 cm (³/₄ in) in from the corners.

2 With right sides of the large piece of felt and the evenweave facing, stitch around three sides, enclosing the tabs at the top and bottom edges.

3 Turn right side out and press. Slip stitch the side opening together and insert sticks through the felt tabs.

4 Attach a piece of cord, which has a tassel tied to each end, to the top stick and use to hang the finished work.

Foxglove mirror back

Pretty dressing-table sets have become popular once again. Make a very special set using this foxglove design.

YOU WILL NEED
Design size: 34 x 59
fabric: 28 hpi evenweave over two
   threads, 20 x 25 cm (8 x 10 in)
26 tapestry needle
stranded cotton, as listed in key
iron
interfacing
craft mirror back
pencil
scissors

Cross stitch in two strands
◇ ◇	858 Light green
▼ ▼	75 Clover pink
∴	271 Light pink
● ●	859 Mid green
△ △	73 Pale pink

Backstitch in one strand
— 78 Very dark pink
— 862 Dark green

French knots in one strand
● 78 Very dark pink

☆ Middle point

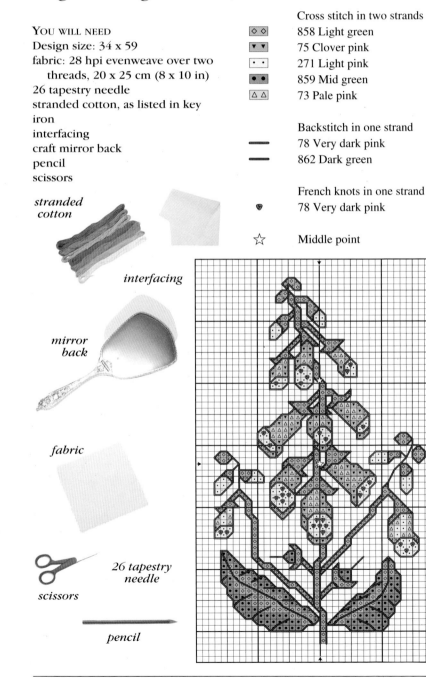

stranded cotton

interfacing

mirror back

fabric

scissors

26 tapestry needle

pencil

1 Starting from the centre of the design, work the foxglove using two strands for cross stitch and one strand for backstitch and French knots.

2 Iron the interfacing on to the back of the embroidery. When complete, position the template supplied with the mirror over the design and trace around it. Cut neatly around the drawn line.

3 Take the mirror apart. Position the embroidery against the metal frame plate and insert the embroidery so that it faces through the opening.

4 Reassemble the mirror.

Pig pot

People love pigs, especially cheeky ones. Surprise a friend by stitching them this charming pot. It'll make their day!

YOU WILL NEED
Design size: 36 x 25
fabric: 18 hpi Aida, 10 x 10 cm
    (4 x 4 in)
26 tapestry needle
stranded cotton, as listed in key
iron
towel
7 cm (2½ in) craft pot
pencil
wadding (batting)
scissors

1 Starting from the centre of the design, work the pig using two strands for cross stitch and one for backstitch and French knots.

2 When the work is complete, check for marks. If it is grubby, you can rinse the stitching in warm, soapy water.

3 Allow it to dry flat and press lightly with the stitching face down on a towel so that you don't flatten the stitches.

4 Mount your work by following the instructions for filling a pot.

pot

stranded cotton

scissors

fabric

wadding (batting)

26 tapestry needle

pencil

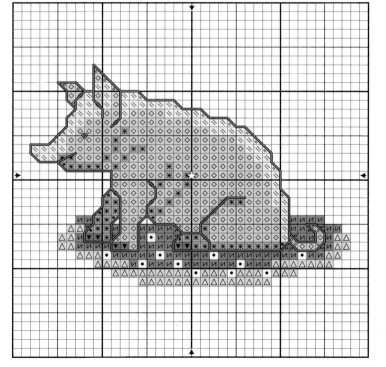

Cross stitch in two strands

✷ ✷	9575 Dark pink
▼ ▼	273 Grey
• •	2 White
⬫ ⬫	1011 Light pink
и и	843 Dark green
◇ ◇	4146 Mid pink
△ △	842 Light green

Backstitch in one strand

— 273 Grey

French knot in one strand

● 273 Grey

☆ Middle point

Summer meadow picture

Conjure up the the beauty of a summer's day with this picture that evokes all the warm, lazy, hazy days of summer.

1 Work the design using two strands for cross stitch and French knots, and one or two strands for backstitch.

2 When the work is complete, check it for marks. If it is grubby, you can rinse the stitching in warm, soapy water.

3 Allow it to dry flat and press lightly with the stitching face down on a towel so that you don't flatten the stitches.

4 Mount your work by following the instructions for lacing a picture.

YOU WILL NEED
Design size: 115 x 78
fabric: 14 hpi Aida, 30 x 20 cm
  (12 x 8 in)
26 tapestry needle
stranded cotton, as listed in key
iron
towel
ruler
pencil
cardboard
wadding (batting)
scissors
pins
sharp needle
sewing thread
picture frame

ruler

scissors

pins

cardboard

stranded cotton

fabric

sharp needle

wadding (batting)

26 tapestry needle

pencil

sewing thread

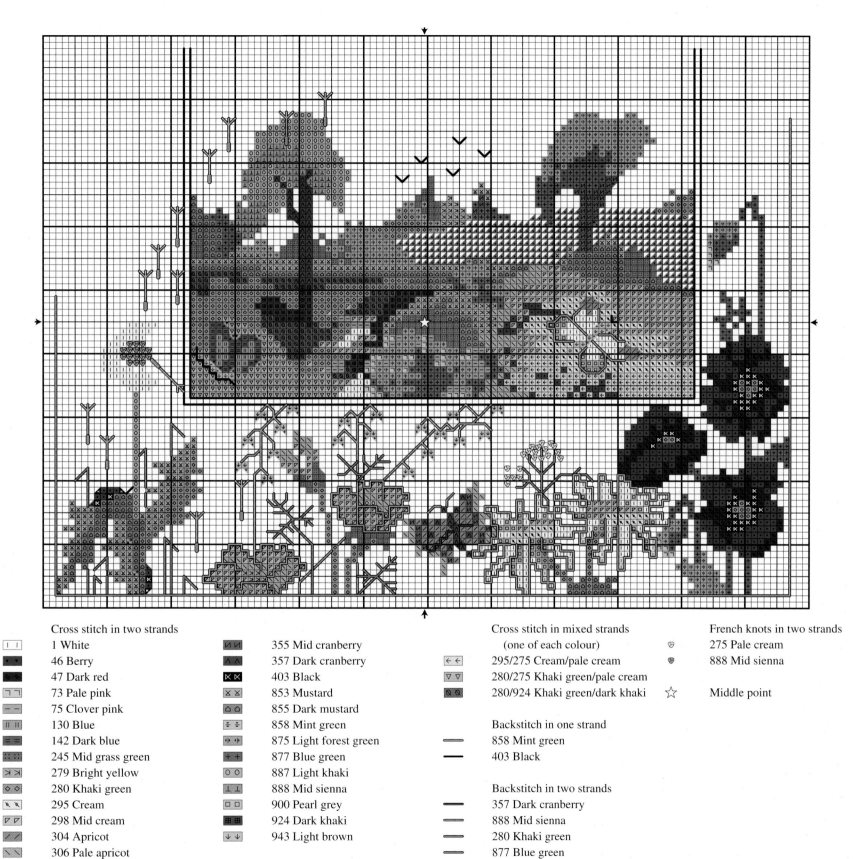

Cross stitch in two strands

| | | 1 White
46 Berry
47 Dark red
73 Pale pink
75 Clover pink
130 Blue
142 Dark blue
245 Mid grass green
279 Bright yellow
280 Khaki green
295 Cream
298 Mid cream
304 Apricot
306 Pale apricot

355 Mid cranberry
357 Dark cranberry
403 Black
853 Mustard
855 Dark mustard
858 Mint green
875 Light forest green
877 Blue green
887 Light khaki
888 Mid sienna
900 Pearl grey
924 Dark khaki
943 Light brown

Cross stitch in mixed strands
(one of each colour)
295/275 Cream/pale cream
280/275 Khaki green/pale cream
280/924 Khaki green/dark khaki

Backstitch in one strand
———— 858 Mint green
———— 403 Black

Backstitch in two strands
———— 357 Dark cranberry
———— 888 Mid sienna
———— 280 Khaki green
———— 877 Blue green

French knots in two strands
275 Pale cream
888 Mid sienna

☆ Middle point

Buttercup cushion

If you hold a buttercup under your chin and your skin reflects the yellow, you are said to be good. Celebrate all things good by making this cushion and displaying it proudly in your home.

YOU WILL NEED

Design size: 120 x 120

fabric: 28 hpi evenweave over two
    threads, 30 x 30 cm (12 x 12 in)

26 tapestry needle

stranded cotton, as listed in key

pins

backing fabric

tape measure

30 cm (12 in) zip (zipper)

sharp needle

sewing thread

scissors

28 cm (11 in) cushion pad

Cross stitch in two strands

266 Light hunter green		269 Very dark hunter green
268 Dark hunter green		1 White
298 Orange		265 Very light hunter green
292 Cream		
289 Bright yellow		**Backstitch in one strand**
297 Mid yellow		269 Very dark hunter green
306 Mid gold	☆	Middle point

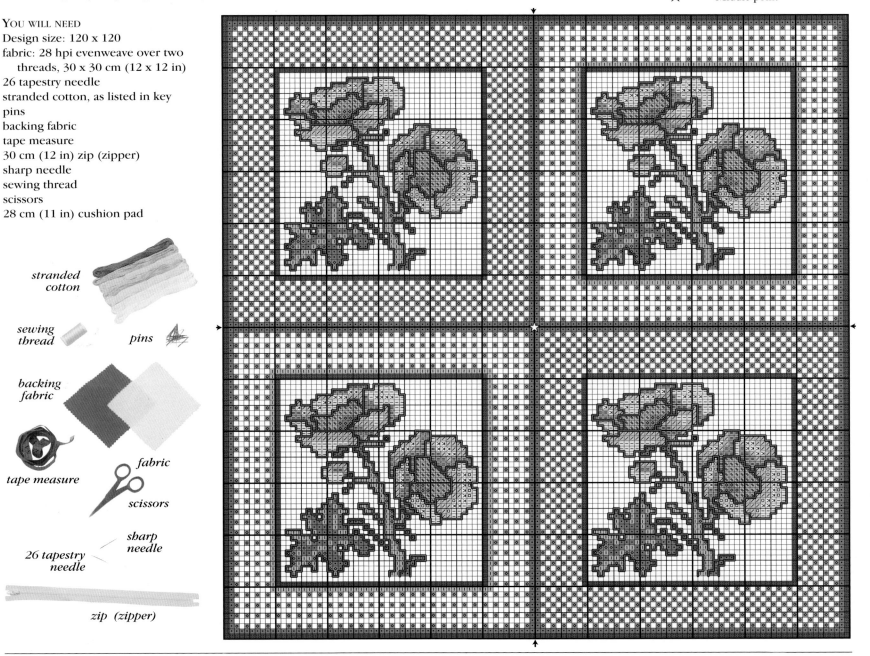

stranded cotton

sewing thread *pins*

backing fabric

tape measure *fabric scissors*

26 tapestry needle *sharp needle*

zip (zipper)

MAKING-UP INSTRUCTIONS

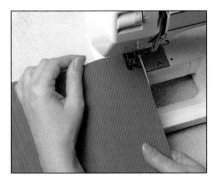

1 Work the design using two strands for cross stitch and one strand for backstitch. Lay the backing fabric over the embroidered piece with right sides facing. Stitch 1 cm (½ in) at either end of the top edge.

2 Insert the zip (zipper). With right sides facing you, place the zip (zipper) behind the fabric. Tack (baste) and stitch the zip (zipper) to the edge of the backing fabric. Then tack (baste) and stitch the front piece to the zip (zipper).

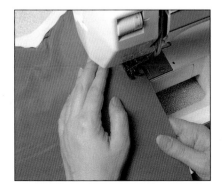

3 Open the zip (zipper) slightly. With right sides facing, stitch around the three open sides. Clip the corners.

4 Unzip the cushion cover and turn it to the right side. Fill the cushion with the cushion pad.

Fox pot

The fox has a mixed reputation – sly and sneaky or clever and endearing. Whatever your viewpoint, this fox design is an attractive project for all nature lovers.

YOU WILL NEED
Design size: 34 x 42
fabric: 18 hpi Aida, 15 x 15 cm
   (6 x 6 in)
26 tapestry needle
stranded cotton, as listed in key
iron
towel
8 cm (3 in) craft pot
pencil
scissors
wadding (batting)

1 Starting from the centre of the design, work the fox using two strands for cross stitch, one strand for the background trees and one for backstitch.

2 When the work is complete, check it for marks. If it is grubby, you can rinse the stitching in warm, soapy water.

3 Allow it to dry flat and press lightly with the stitching face down on a towel so that you don't flatten the stitches.

4 Mount your work by following the instructions for filling a pot.

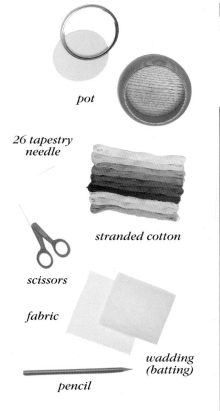

pot

26 tapestry needle

stranded cotton

scissors

fabric

wadding (batting)

pencil

Cross stitch in two strands

■	403 Black
+ +	842 Light green
▽ ▽	886 Dark cream
• •	926 Cream
/ /	347 Light rust
✳ ✳	349 Brown
▼ ▼	351 Mid mink
◇ ◇	843 Dark green

Cross stitch in one strand

↑ ↑	379 Mid beige
∧ ∧	376 Light beige

Backstitch in one strand
— 1050 Dark brown

☆ Middle point

Doves in cote card

Delicate pastel shades make this card calm and gentle. The doves represent peace, so giving this card is a true sign of friendship.

YOU WILL NEED
Design size: 42 x 70
fabric: 14 hpi Aida, 10 cm x 15 cm
  (4 x 6 in)
26 tapestry needle
stranded cotton, as listed in key
iron
towel
card with opening
pencil
wadding (batting)
scissors
double-sided tape

Cross stitch in two strands
27 Deep rose pink
23 Pink
1048 Mid rust
276 Deep cream
9159 Pale blue
206 Sea green
293 Yellow
235 Slate grey
234 Pearl grey
275 Pale cream

Backstitch in one strand
235 Slate grey

☆ Middle point

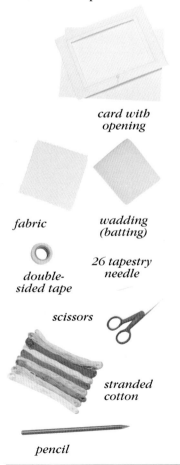

card with opening

fabric

wadding (batting)

double-sided tape

26 tapestry needle

scissors

stranded cotton

pencil

1 Starting from the centre of the design, work the motif using two strands for cross stitch and one for backstitch.

2 When the work is complete, check it for marks. If it is grubby, you can rinse the stitching in warm, soapy water.

3 Allow it to dry flat and press lightly with the stitching face down on a towel so that you don't flatten the stitches.

4 Mount your work by following the instructions for filling a card.

Deer and fawn picture

In the forest the deer grazes with its fawn by its side. Mother and baby peek out from the safety of their woodland home.

1 Work your design using two strands for cross stitch and backstitch, and one for half cross stitch and French knots.

2 When the work is complete, check it for marks. If it is grubby, you can rinse the stitching in warm, soapy water.

3 Allow it to dry flat and press lightly with the stitching face down on a towel so that you don't flatten the stitches.

4 Mount your work by following the instructions for lacing a picture.

YOU WILL NEED
Design size: 120 x 113
fabric: 14 hpi natural Aida,
   30 x 28 cm (12 x 11 in)
26 tapestry needle
stranded cotton, as listed in key
iron
towel
ruler
pencil
cardboard
wadding (batting)
scissors
pins
sharp needle
sewing thread
picture frame

ruler

stranded cotton

scissors

pins

sewing thread

cardboard

26 tapestry needle

fabric

needle

wadding (batting)

pencil

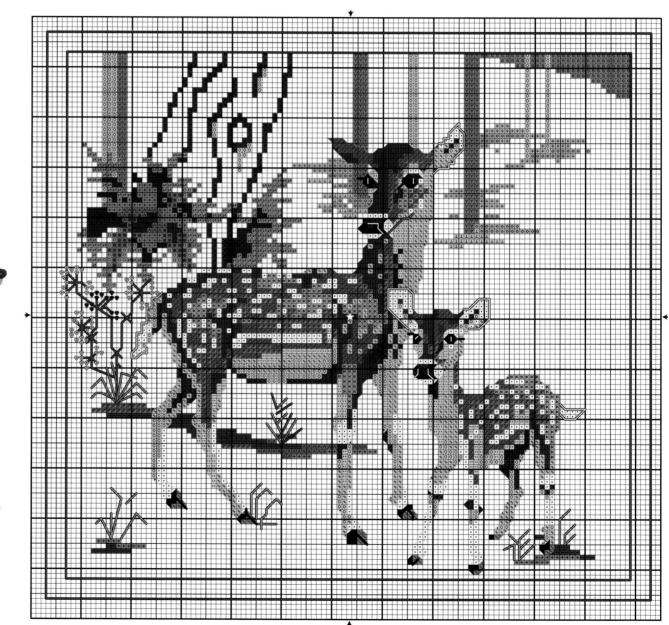

72

Cross stitch in two strands

�· �·	275 Pale cream
�markslash	276 Cream
+ +	308 Dark gold
▬ ▬	310 Mid brown
I I	351 Mid mink
····	361 Light brown
⋈ ⋈	363 Mid tan
■	403 Black
O O	831 Dark cream
⊥ ⊥	874 Light sage green
□ □	887 Light forest green
⊞ ⊞	888 Mid sienna
▦ ▦	889 Dark brown
▶ ▶	898 Dark forest brown
◇ ◇	907 Mid brown
◣ ◣	1041 Very dark brown
▽ ▽	1048 Mid rust
⁄ ⁄	1049 Rust
▨ ▨	8581 Slate grey

Cross stitch in mixed strands
    (one of each colour)

И И	361/363 Light brown/mid tan
∧ ∧	308/310 Dark gold/mid brown
⋉ ⋉	363/1049 Mid tan/rust
Y Y	898/831 Dark forest brown/ dark cream

Half cross stitch in one strand
    (background)

S S	850 Slate blue
÷ ÷	907 Mid forest green

Backstitch in two strands

──	310 Mid brown
──	831 Dark cream
──	888 Mid sienna
──	1049 Rust
──	403 Black
──	1 White

French knots in one strand

●	363 Mid tan
♲	306 Mid gold

☆	Middle point

Cyclamen footstool cover

Footstools provide the opportunity for creating a wide range of cross-stitch designs. This cyclamen design is relatively easy to stitch and would make a good project for a beginner to try.

	Cross stitch in two strands		Backstitch in one strand
▼ ▼	87 Dark pink	—	879 Very dark forest green
o o	214 Light green	—	1029 Very dark pink
⊞ ⊞	217 Dark leaf green		
● ●	215 Light leaf green	☆	Middle point
· ·	85 Light pink		
△ △	86 Mid pink		

YOU WILL NEED
Design size: 110 x110
fabric: 14 hpi Aida, 36 x 36 cm
 (14 x 14 in)
26 tapestry needle
stranded cotton, as listed in key
pencil
tape measure
scissors
sharp needle
sewing thread
28 cm (11 in) craft footstool
screwdriver

stranded cotton

footstool

scissors

pencil

26 tapestry needle

sharp needle

sewing thread

tape measure

fabric

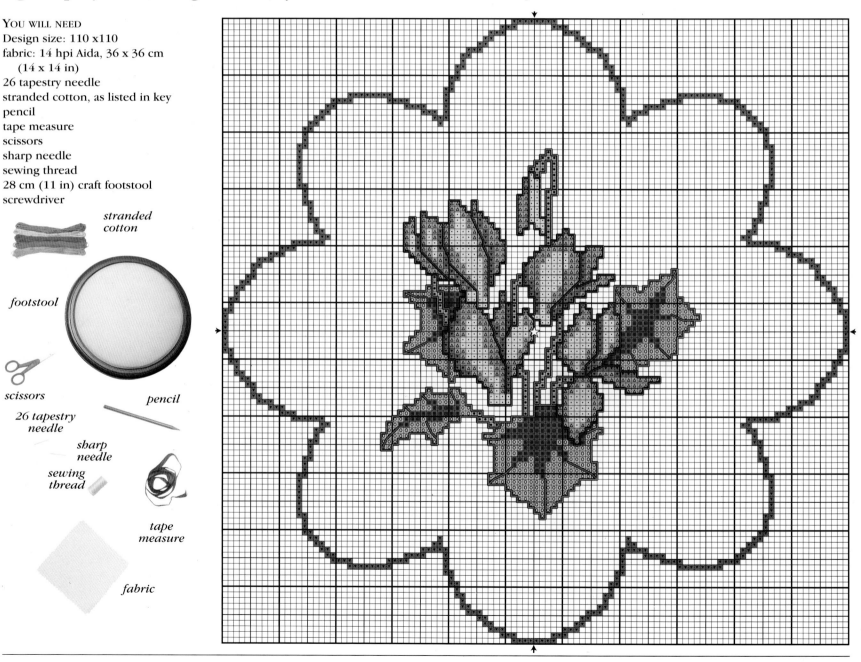

MAKING-UP INSTRUCTIONS

1 Work the design using two strands for cross stitch and one for backstitch. When complete, draw a 36 cm (14 in) circle around it and cut it out.

2 Run a double gathering stitch 6 mm (¹/₄ in) inside the raw edge of the fabric.

3 Remove the pad from the footstool and place the design face up on the pad. Pull the gathering threads, adjusting the design as you go so that it remains in the centre of the stool.

4 Using a screwdriver, fix the base back on to the stool.

Squirrel paperweight

Furry woodland creatures such as squirrels make good cross-stitch designs and people enjoy receiving them.

YOU WILL NEED
Design size: 35 x 34
fabric: 18 hpi Aida, 10 x 10 cm
    (4 x 4 in)
26 tapestry needle
stranded cotton, as listed in key
8 cm (3 in) craft paperweight
pencil
scissors

1 First work the design using one strand throughout.

2 When complete, draw around the piece of felt supplied with the paperweight on to your design, centring the motif.

3 Cut neatly around the drawn line on the design.

4 Place the embroidery under the paperweight with the design facing into the glass and finish by placing the sticky felt on the bottom.

pencil

paperweight

tape measure

26 tapestry needle

stranded cotton

scissors

fabric

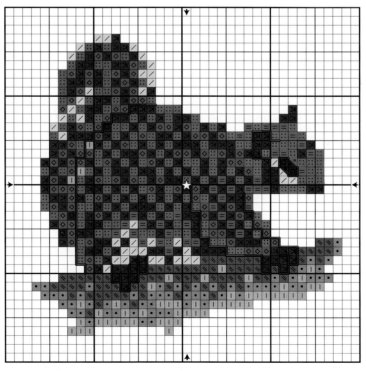

Cross stitch in one strand
273 Mid grey brown
8581 Stone grey
845 Sage
382 Chocolate brown
390 Cream
355 Claret brown
400 Slate grey
905 Mink brown
1041 Deep slate grey

Backstitch in one strand
905 Mink brown

☆   Middle point

TIP

If you wrap the edges of your fabric before stitching, with either masking tape or a zigzag stitch, it will prevent the fabric snagging or fraying while you are stitching it.

Mushrooms in basket card

This motif could also be used to decorate an apron or recipe box. It is a colourful kitchen design that looks great on a greetings card.

YOU WILL NEED
Design size: 43 x 60
fabric: 14 hpi Aida plus, 10 x 13 cm
(4 x 5 in)
26 tapestry needle
stranded cotton, as listed in key
iron
towel
card with opening
pencil
wadding (batting)
scissors
double-sided tape

1 Starting from the centre of the design, work the motif using two strands for cross stitch and one strand for backstitch.

2 When the work is complete, check it for marks. If it is grubby, you can rinse the stitching in warm, soapy water.

3 Allow it to dry flat and press lightly with the stitching face down on a towel so that you don't flatten the stitches.

4 Mount your work by following the instructions for filling a card.

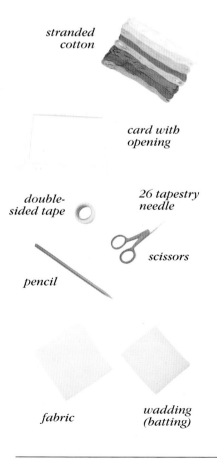

stranded cotton

card with opening

double-sided tape

26 tapestry needle

scissors

pencil

fabric

wadding (batting)

Cross stitch in two strands

	1	White
	306	Mid gold
	886	Beige
	889	Dark brown
	214	Light green
	218	Dark green
	19	Claret red

Backstitch in one strand
236 Dark grey

☆ Middle point

Swan purse

Keep your pennies safe in this useful purse. Easy
to stitch and easy to make up, it's a design anyone
could try successfully.

YOU WILL NEED
Design size: 70 x 62
fabric: 14 hpi Aida, 15 x 15 cm
    (6 x 6 in)
26 tapestry needle
stranded cotton, as listed in key
backing fabric
tape measure
sewing thread
sharp needle
pins
10 cm (4 in) zip (zipper)
scissors

scissors

*stranded
cotton*

needle

*backing
fabric*

*26 tapestry
needle*

pins

*sewing
thread*

*zip
(zipper)*

*tape
measure*

fabric

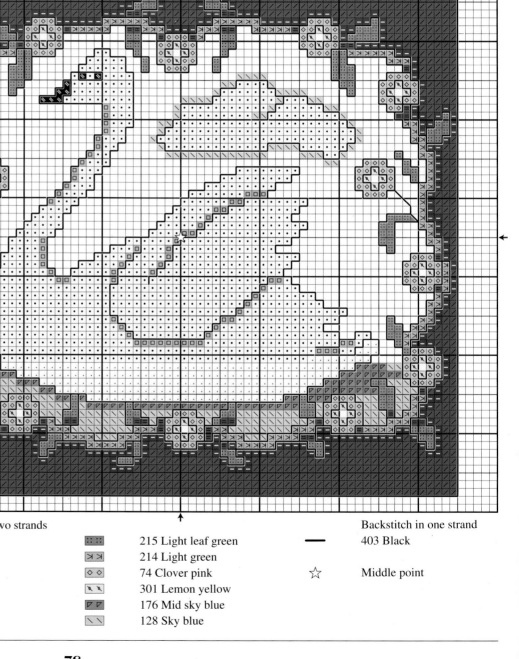

Cross stitch in two strands			Backstitch in one strand
· · 1 White	▦ 215 Light leaf green		— 403 Black
403 Black	◤◤ 214 Light green		
□ □ 397 Pearl grey	◇ ◇ 74 Clover pink		☆ Middle point
– – 127 Royal blue	🔦 🔦 301 Lemon yellow		
◢ ◢ 979 Navy blue	▽ ▽ 176 Mid sky blue		
▬ ▬ 218 Dark green	◻ ◻ 128 Sky blue		

MAKING-UP INSTRUCTIONS

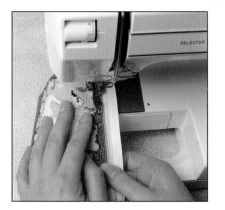

1 Work the design using two strands for cross stitch and one strand for backstitch. Lay the backing fabric over the embroidered fabric with right sides facing. Stitch 1 cm (½ in) at either end of the top edge.

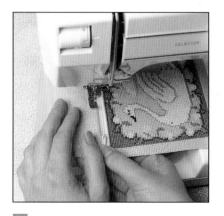

2 Insert the zip (zipper). With right sides facing you, place the zip (zipper) behind the fabric. Tack (baste) and stitch the zip (zipper) to the edge of the backing fabric. Then tack (baste) and stitch the front piece to the zip (zipper).

3 Open the zip (zipper) slightly. With right sides facing, stitch around the three open sides.

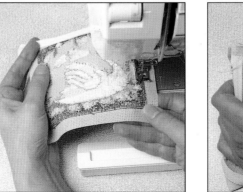

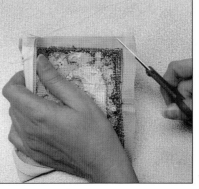

4 Clip the corners and turn the purse right side out.

Owl apron

Cheer up a plain apron by stitching a quirky design on to the front. This cheeky owl is great fun to stitch.

YOU WILL NEED
Design size: 56 x 55
fabric: 14 hpi Aida, 13 x 13 cm
  (5 x 5 in)
26 tapestry needle
stranded cotton, as listed in key
sharp needle
apron
scissors
sewing thread
pins

apron

Cross stitch in two strands
350 Deep pink
3340 Deep apricot
725 Mid beige
906 Bright green
830 Dark brown
677 Cream
729 Dark cream
300 Reddish-brown
415 Pearl grey
310 Black
001 White

Backstitch in one strand
—— 310 Black
—— 986 Dark forest green
—— 840 Mid brown

French knot in two strands
403 Black

☆   Middle point

stranded cotton

tape measure

sewing thread

pins

26 tapestry needle

needle

fabric

scissors

MAKING-UP INSTRUCTIONS

1 Work the design using two strands for cross stitch and French knots, and one strand for backstitch. Turn under the edges of the design by about 1 cm (¹/₂ in) and tack (baste) them in place.

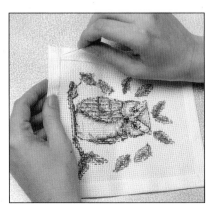

2 Position the design on the front of the apron.

3 Tack (baste) it on to the front of the apron front ready for stitching.

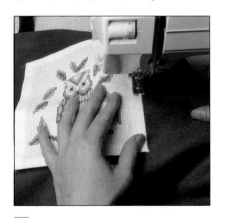

4 Sew around the design using a straight stitch. Alternatively, you could zigzag over the edges of the design. Trim away any loose threads.

Autumn scene

Recall the dazzling hues of a crisp autumnal day with this esoteric design.

YOU WILL NEED
Design size: 49 x 68
fabric: 14 hpi natural Aida,
    18 x 23 cm (7 x 9 in)
26 tapestry needle
stranded cotton, as listed in key
iron
towel
ruler
pencil
cardboard
wadding (batting)
scissors
pins
sharp needle
sewing thread
picture frame

1 Work the design using two strands for cross stitch and one for backstitch.

2 When the work is complete, check it for marks. If it is grubby, you can rinse the stitching in warm, soapy water.

3 Allow it to dry flat and press lightly with the stitching face down on a towel so that you don't flatten the stitches.

4 Mount your work by following the instructions for lacing a picture.

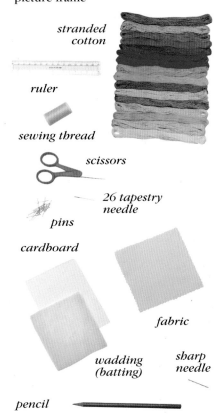

stranded cotton

ruler

sewing thread

scissors

26 tapestry needle

pins

cardboard

fabric

wadding (batting)

sharp needle

pencil

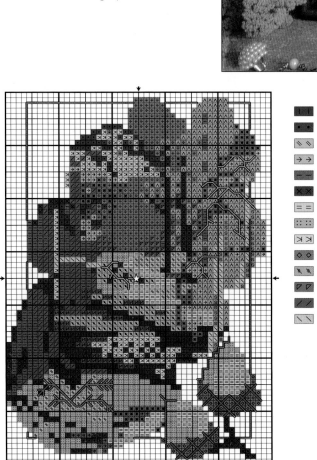

Cross stitch in two strands

I I	19 Claret red	И И	1014 Light berry red
• •	46 Berry red	∧ ∧	1047 Mid beige
∖ ∖	280 Mid grass green	✳ ✳	1048 Mid peach
→ →	298 Deep yellow	Y Y	5975 Deep russet
▬ ▬	349 Mid rust	S S	8581 Charcoal grey
✕ ✕	357 Deep rust	≑ ≑	977 Sky blue
═ ═	361 Yellow cream	╫ ╫	1024 Deep pink
⋮ ⋮	363 Mid tan		
↘ ↘	376 Light grey		Backstitch in one strand
◇ ◇	379 Mid beige	——	877 Grass green
◹ ◹	868 Light sienna	——	889 Dark brown
▽ ▽	877 Grass green	——	1014 Light berry red
∕ ∕	889 Dark brown	——	8581 Charcoal grey
∖ ∖	900 Mid grey		
		☆	Middle point

Pears table set

Make a complete set of napkins and napkin holders. The pear design is easy and quick to stitch and will add a unique touch to your table.

YOU WILL NEED

Design size: 20 x 21

fabric: 18 hpi Aida and 14 hpi waste canvas

26 tapestry needle

stranded cotton, as listed in key

craft napkin holder

napkin

sharp needle

sewing thread

scissors

tweezers (optional)

1 For the napkin holder, work the design on the Aida using one strand throughout. Insert the finished design into the napkin holder.

2 For the napkin, adapt the pear motif to make a new design, or simply use the same pattern as on the napkin holder. Tack (baste) a piece of waste canvas on to the napkin where you want the design to appear.

3 Work the design through both the napkin and the waste canvas using two strands for cross stitch and one strand for backstitch.

4 To remove the waste canvas, just lightly dampen your work. As the canvas softens, you can remove it thread by thread. This may be easier to do with a pair of tweezers.

napkin

stranded cotton

fabric

craft napkin holder

scissors

26 tapestry needle

tape measure

pencil

sharp needle

sewing thread

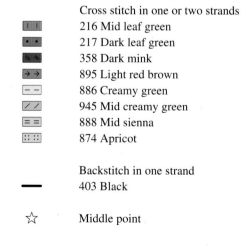

Cross stitch in one or two strands

216 Mid leaf green

217 Dark leaf green

358 Dark mink

895 Light red brown

886 Creamy green

945 Mid creamy green

888 Mid sienna

874 Apricot

Backstitch in one strand

— 403 Black

☆ Middle point

Robin needlecase

Stuck for ideas for Christmas presents? If so, why not make this practical and attractive needlecase? It's an easy project for a beginner and people love receiving handmade gifts.

YOU WILL NEED
Design size: 27 x 26
fabric: 28 hpi evenweave over two
    threads, four pieces 11 x 10 cm
    (4½ x 4 in)
26 tapestry needle
stranded cotton, as listed in key
iron
interfacing
tape measure
sharp needle
sewing thread
pins
felt
scissors

stranded cotton

interfacing

tape measure

26 tapestry needle

needle

scissors

sewing thread

fabric

pins

felt

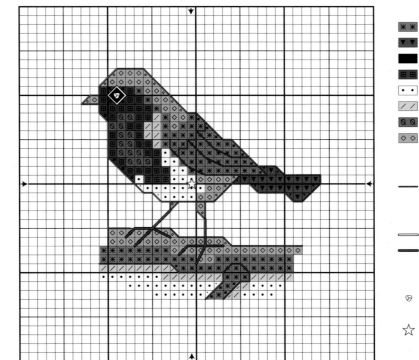

Cross stitch in two strands
349 Brown
351 Mid mink
403 Black
9046 Dark red
2 White
234 Grey
335 Light red
347 Light brown

Backstitch in one strand
352 Very dark brown

Backstitch in two strands
2 White
352 Very dark brown

French knot in one strand
2 White

☆ Middle point

MAKING-UP INSTRUCTIONS

1 Work the design on one of the pieces of evenweave using two strands for cross stitch and some backstitch, and one strand for French knots and remaining backstitch. Iron interfacing to the back of the embroidered piece and one other piece of evenweave. Lay each piece with interfacing on one of the remaining evenweave pieces and, with right sides facing, stitch along two long edges and one short edge.

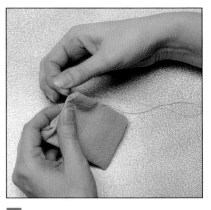

2 Turn both pieces right sides out and press. Slip stitch the open edge together.

3 Place the two pieces together with a slightly smaller piece of felt between. Stitch through all three layers by hand.

TIP
You can use any of the smaller motifs in this book to decorate needlecases, towels, tablecloths and table linen.

Pine cone card

Cross-stitch Christmas cards are always well received. This pine cone card suggests a winter countryside, but is refreshingly unlike traditional Christmas scenes.

YOU WILL NEED
Design size: 31 x 40
fabric: 14 hpi Aida, 10 x 10 cm
    (4 x 4 in)
26 tapestry needle
stranded cotton, as listed in key
iron
towel
card with opening
pencil
wadding (batting)
scissors
double-sided tape

1 Starting from the centre of the design, work the pine cone using two strands for cross stitch and one strand for backstitch.

2 When the work is complete, check it for marks. If it is grubby, you can rinse the stitching in warm, soapy water.

3 Allow it to dry flat and press lightly with the stitching face down on a towel so that you don't flatten the stitches.

4 Mount your work by following the instructions for filling a card.

card with opening

stranded cotton

26 tapestry needle

pencil

scissors

fabric

wadding (batting)

double-sided tape

Cross stitch in two strands
391 Mushroom
393 Very dark brown
905 Mink brown

Backstitch in one strand
236 Dark grey
879 Very dark forest green
905 Mink brown

☆ Middle point

Holly and berries tree decoration

Cross-stitch tree decorations will make your Christmas tree stand out from the crowd this year. Why not set yourself a challenge and complete a whole set of decorations?

YOU WILL NEED
Design size: 37 x 36
fabric: 14 hpi Aida, 10 x 10 cm (4 x 4 in)
26 tapestry needle
stranded cotton, as listed in key
pencil
tape measure
scissors
sharp needle
sewing thread
8 cm (3 in) embroidery frame
felt

Cross stitch in two strands
1044 Dark grass green
246 Mid grass green
245 Privet green
47 Dark red
46 Berry red
307 Gold
298 Deep yellow

Backstitch in one strand
246 Mid grass green
47 Dark red
307 Gold

☆ Middle point

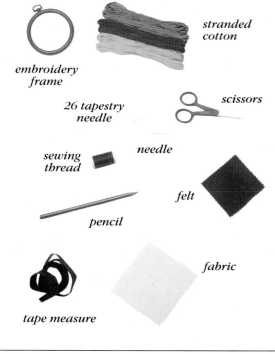

embroidery frame

stranded cotton

26 tapestry needle

scissors

sewing thread

needle

pencil

felt

tape measure

fabric

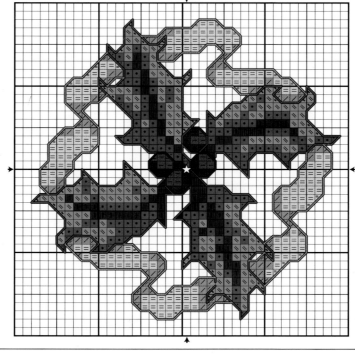

1 Work the design using two strands for cross stitch and one strand for backstitch. When complete, draw a 10 cm (4 in) circle around the design and cut it out.

2 Run a double gathering stitch 6 mm (¹/₄ in) inside the raw edge of the fabric. Position the design over the inside rim of the 8 cm (3 in) embroidery frame and draw up the gathering thread, ensuring that the design remains in the centre of the frame.

3 Lace the design into the back of the frame and replace the outside ring over the frame.

4 Finish by slip stitching a circle of felt over the back of your work.

Mistletoe bookmark

This bookmark is quick and easy to make. Placed inside a friend's favourite book, it will make a unique gift.

YOU WILL NEED
Design size: 26 x 110
fabric: 14 hpi Aida plus, 7.5 x 23 cm
  (3 x 9 in)
24 tapestry needle
stranded cotton, as listed in key
scissors
tape measure
sharp needle
sewing thread
ribbon

1 Work the design using two strands for cross stitch and one for backstitch. Cut around the finished design.

2 To make the tassel, cut seven lengths of light green Marlitt about 20 cm (8 in) long. Fold them in half to make a loop at the top.

3 Wrap a long thread around the threads just below the loop and stitch it through the threads. Stitch your tassel to the bottom of the bookmark.

4 To finish, slip stitch a piece of ribbon behind the bookmark. Trim to match the shape of the bookmark.

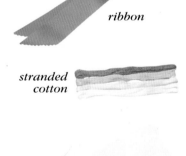

ribbon

stranded cotton

Cross stitch in two strands
205 Mid mint green
1042 Mint green
275 Mid cream
001 White

Backstitch in one strand
1042 Mint green
258 Dark mint green

☆ Middle point

scissors

fabric

24 tapestry needle

sewing thread

needle

tape measure

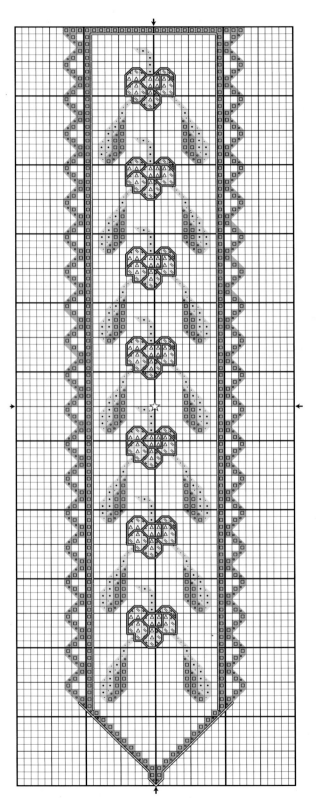

Snow scene birthday book

A birthday book is always a welcome gift. Make it appropriate for winter by filling it with a moody snow scene.

YOU WILL NEED
Design size: 45 x 57
fabric: 28 hpi evenweave over two
    threads, 15 x 20 cm (6 x 8 in)
26 tapestry needle
stranded cotton, as listed in key
iron
interfacing
pencil
scissors
craft birthday book
double-sided tape

craft birthday book

stranded cotton

double-sided tape

26 tapestry needle

scissors

interfacing

pencil

fabric

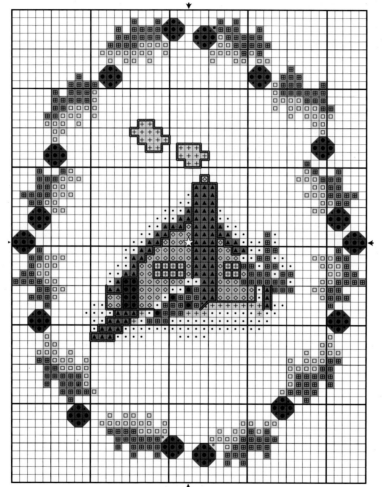

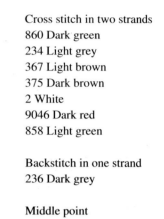

Cross stitch in two strands

⊞ ⊞	860 Dark green
+ +	234 Light grey
◇ ◇	367 Light brown
▲ ▲	375 Dark brown
· ·	2 White
● ●	9046 Dark red
☐ ☐	858 Light green

Backstitch in one strand

——	236 Dark grey

☆	Middle point

1 Work the design using two strands for cross stitch and one for backstitch.

2 Iron interfacing on to the back of the design.

3 Cut the fabric to fit the book.

4 Slide the design into the front pocket of the book and fix with double-sided tape.

TIP

When you start stitching avoid starting with a knot. If you are mounting your work against a flat surface, the knot will put pressure against the fabric and in time will weaken that area of material. Instead, bring your needle up through the fabric, leaving a tail at the back of your work. When making the first few stitches ensure you work them over the loose tail. These stitches will hold the thread firmly. To finish a length of thread, take it to the back of the work and thread the needle through the back of the last few stitches that were made. Cut the thread.

Spider in web card

On cold, frosty mornings, when the sparkling frost transforms the leaves and grass, the spider's web gleams like diamonds.

YOU WILL NEED
Design size: 32 x 43
fabric: 14 hpi Aida, 10 x 15 cm
    (4 x 6 in)
26 tapestry needle
stranded cotton, as listed in key
iron
towel
card with opening
pencil
wadding (batting)
scissors
double-sided tape

1 Starting from the centre of the design, work the motif using two strands for cross stitch, two strands for backstitch on the legs and one strand for all remaining backstitch.

2 When the work is complete, check it for marks. If it is grubby, you can rinse the stitching in warm, soapy water.

3 Allow it to dry flat and press lightly with the stitching face down on a towel so that you don't flatten the stitches.

4 Mount your work by following the instructions for filling a card.

card with opening

stranded cotton

Kreinik silver cord

double-sided tape

26 tapestry needle

pencil

scissors

fabric

wadding (batting)

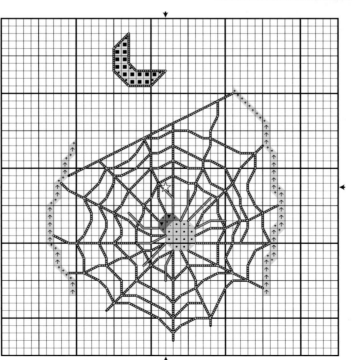

Cross stitch in two strands
234 Light grey
235 Dark grey
254 Dark yellow-green
386 Cream

Backstitch in two strands
234 Light grey

Backstitch in one strand
001C Kreinik silver cord

French knot in two strands
234 Light grey

☆ Middle point

Badger pot

Big and sturdy, slow and methodical, the badger is still quite a rare sight and certainly one to remember.

YOU WILL NEED
Design size: 37 x 33
fabric: 18 hpi Aida, 10 x 10 cm
   (4 x 4 in)
26 tapestry needle
stranded cotton, as listed in key
iron
towel
7 cm (2½ in) craft pot
pencil
scissors
wadding (batting)

1 Starting from the centre of the design, work the motif using two strands for cross stitch and dark green backstitch, and one strand for French knots and remaining backstitch.

2 When the work is complete, check it for marks. If it is grubby, you can rinse the stitching in warm, soapy water.

3 Allow it to dry flat and press lightly with the stitching face down on a towel so that you don't flatten the stitches.

4 Mount your work by following the instructions for filling a pot.

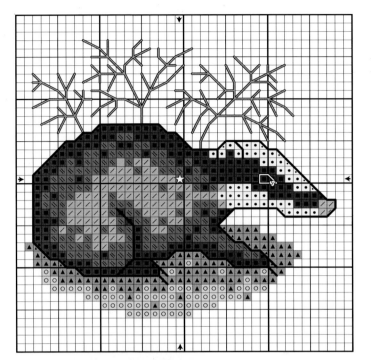

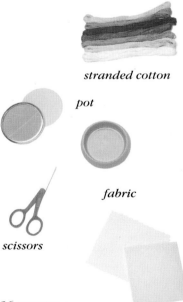

stranded cotton

pot

fabric

scissors

26 tapestry needle

wadding (batting)

pencil

Cross stitch in two strands
236 Dark grey
399 Light grey
842 Light green
843 Dark green
2 White
235 Mid grey

Backstitch in one strand
403 Black
2 White

Backstitch in two strands
843 Dark green

French knot in one strand
2 White

☆ Middle point

Mice clock

In "Hickory Dickory Dock" the mouse ran up the clock. In this design, cute mice run around the clock. This is an ideal beginner's project.

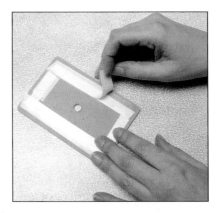

YOU WILL NEED
Design size: 58 x 84
fabric: 18 hpi Aida, 15 x 13 cm
  (6 x 5 in)
26 tapestry needle
stranded cotton, as listed in key
double-sided tape
small craft clock

MAKING-UP INSTRUCTIONS

1 Work the design using two strands for cross stitch and French knots, and one strand for backstitch. Attach double-sided tape around the edges of the piece of cardboard supplied with the clock.

2 Place the design face down on a flat surface and place the cardboard on top with the double-sided tape uppermost. Stick the edges on to the cardboard.

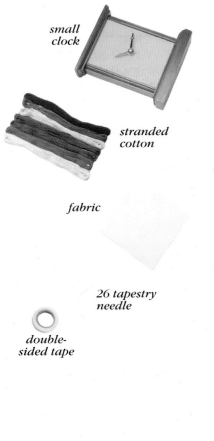

small clock

stranded cotton

fabric

26 tapestry needle

double-sided tape

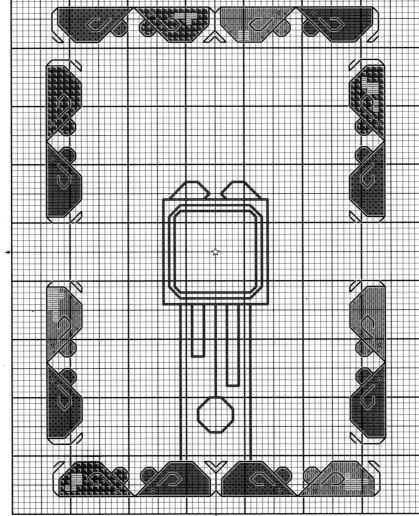

Cross stitch in two strands
936 Mid brown
1041 Dark grey
1046 Mid reddish-brown
234 Pearl grey
387 Mid cream

Backstitch in one strand
—— 403 Black
—— 905 Mink brown

French knot in two strands
● 403 Black

☆ Middle point

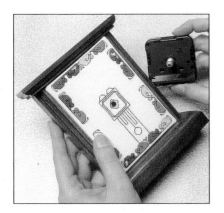

3 Place the design in the clock frame facing outwards. Fix the clock movement into the back of the clock.

4 To finish, attach the hands.

TIP

You can use double-sided tape to fix your work to the back of a board before framing. It is satisfactory as a temporary measure, or on something you don't expect to last. For a more permanent method, follow the instructions for lacing a picture.

212 0551. *Mail order suppliers of miniatures and cards.*

Contributors

The Publishers are grateful to the following contributors whose work appears in this book:
Alison Burton: Otter pot; Rabbit coaster; Hedgehog pot; Dragonfly card; Squirrel paperweight; Pears table set; Pine cone card; Holly and berries tree decoration.
Christine Coggan: Aconites sampler (design).
Lesley Grant: Fledglings picture; Kingfisher shopping bag; Bees padded coat hanger; Summer meadow picture; Deer and fawn picture; Autumn scene.
Maureen Kennaugh: Peacock book cover; Honeysuckle café curtain border design; Butterfly shoulder-bag.
Dawn Parmley: Swan purse; Owl apron.
Penelope Randall: Frogs on waterlilies tray cloth; Corn-cob pot; Doves in cote card.
Jane Rimmer: Duckling school gym bag; Daisy shelf border.
Barbara Smith: Lavender hat band; Mice clock.
Zoë Smith: Bluebells cushion; Primrose picture frame; Buttercup cushion.
Julia Tidmarsh: Violet glasses case; Apple-blossom coffee pot cover; Trout print; Swallows pot; Rainbow bookmark; Ladybird paperweight; Golden pheasant cabinet; Foxglove mirror back; Oak tree hanging; Pig pot; Cyclamen footstool cover; Robin needlecase; Spider in web card; Badger pot; Fox pot; Snow scene birthday book; Aconites sampler (stitching).
Lynda Whittle: Heron card; Wild rose card; Mushrooms in basket card; Mistletoe bookmark.

Publisher's Acknowledgments

The Publishers are grateful to the following companies who supplied materials used for photography:

Coats Crafts UK
PO Box 22, The Lingfield Estate, McMullen Road, Darlington, County Durham, DL1 1YQ, 01325 394 394. *Suppliers of Anchor embroidery threads.*

Framecraft Miniatures Limited
372/376 Summer Lane, Hockley, Birmingham, B19 3QA. Tel: 0121